CHURCHES

INCORPORATED

Looking Behind the Cross
Looking Beyond the Cross

James E. Alston

 page vision

228 Hamilton Ave.,
Palo Alto, CA 94301

Copyright © 2023 by James E. Alston.

ISBN 978-1-960946-02-7 (softcover)
ISBN 978-1-960946-03-4 (hardcover)
ISBN 978-1-960946-04-1 (ebook)

Printed in the United States of America.

DEDICATION

This book is dedicated to my father, the late James Alston Sr., and my beloved and devout grandmother, Ms. Annie C. Thomas. My grandmother loaned the church twenty-five hundred dollars of her savings to bind a contract to purchase a building that stands today, housing the corporate ministry. What's more, I devote this book to the celebration of birth and the life of little Jordan Denise Alexander–Alston, my great niece. Jordan has a purpose and importance to our family legacy.

In commemoration of Andrea Taylor–Benjamin. A percentage of this book sale will be donated to the American Cancer Society.

ACKNOWLEDGMENT

THIS BOOK IS INTENDED FOR the churches' brokenhearted, the over-churched, and under-churched. This text tells us how to care about each other through God's grace principles. A broken corporate church relationship will never leave an individual the same; however, it is possible to mend the heart. Some broken church relationships are beyond repair, and there is no going back. You put your heart, mind, soul, body, and money into an organization you truly believed in. Just to be let down and disappointed by your church's corporate leadership. You tried to stay, but you just could not continue to bear the weight of your own hurt and embarrassment while witnessing the pain of others. Brokenhearted Christians are then unmindfully considered to be backsliders. I've seen how hurting people can hurt people.

Countless thanks and heartfelt appreciation to my editors:

Ms. Karen I. Prestwidge, MS
Ms. Dyhanne C. Terrell–Alston, MS
Ms. Jean Lynn Walker, MS

I, in particular, acknowledge Bishop Michelle White-Haynes, the pastor of Greater Faith Temple Church. Pastor White is a legend to exemplary biblical principles by her own right, and committed to keeping it real. I hold enormous gratitude to Bishop Michelle White-Haynes.

Please keep in mind this text is about church corporate leadership regimes. It is not about a Higher Power.

CONTENTS

PREFACE

CHURCHES INCORPORATED WILL TAKE YOU into a setting with eye-opening experiences. Who are the people behind the crosses they wear? Be prepared to embark on a journey and subject matter that your Sunday school won't teach, your weekly Bible class avoids, and your preacher will by no means talk about. This journey and destination will leave you riveted to what you know, what you don't know, and what you thought you knew. When a minister errors, show them the love and the human side of us. Let them feel they can reach for the *mea culpa* and still maintain respected authority within our lives. "Absolute faith corrupts as absolutely as absolute power" (Eric Hoffer).

INTRODUCTION

My intent for writing this book is to correct a moral wrong. The church corporation and some names have been changed to protect the innocent and unsuspecting. I bring nothing new except a desire for church transparency and for churches to step up their game. Congregations, in turn, should not require their ministers to walk on water. Instead, lift them up in prayer. Let's not forget that ministers are human. We must encourage our ministers to do the right thing through respectful accountability. Churches supply so many with a beacon of hope and a ray of sunshine. It bothers me when believers invest their mind, heart, soul, money, and faith into a church, only then to be exploited by the leadership regime.

When I see and think of parishioners with broken hearts, I think of how many sermons professed or people around proclaimed, "Keep on keeping on, I am praying for you, no matter what, don't stop coming." Gradually, all the things you were taught from this corporate ministry start to become paper-thin and fluid, leaving you adrift. You begin to feel isolated from the people you worshiped with so closely. The voices that were once warm, soothing, and nonthreatening are now announcing your peril and fate. Many corporate church leadership regimes leave their followers feeling demeaned, invalidated, and suppressed. How? By silencing them. They take away your voice. When you find the courage to listen to your quiet inner voice, which tells you it's time to leave, you go with a numbing feeling, left with memories, but not feeling whole. You try to fill the void with different people, another church. Slowly you start to understand your only hope is a Higher Power. Your faith will carry you to a higher place that will fill the void and mend the hurt.

At some point you begin to understand that your spiritual and emotional safety and well-being are based on a power outside of your own. You take on a renewed responsibility for your actions. You notice your self-esteem begins to soar. You begin to interpret and understand the love of a Higher Power. You move toward a spirituality that is not based on moments of synthetic mass hysteria enclosed in brick and mortar. You become a true spiritual being. This book will help to understand the inherent ambiguity and the inner workings of corporate church leadership regimes. Churches, in and of themselves, are a symbol of our right to worship the way we choose.

Are corporate church leadership regimes exploiting their flocks? Have churches become incapable of preparing us for the day of Judgment by abstaining from *fearmongering, intimidation, and religious rules laced with legalistic doctrines?* The CNN News Broadcast reported on February 11, 2013, that Atheists, for the first time in history, are growing at a faster rate than Christianity. To those who remain dedicated to the service of a corporate church leadership regime, may the fundamental truth of what you believe and who you believe in continue to stand the test of time.

WHAT EXACTLY IS GOING ON HERE?

I walked through the wood frame glass pane double doors into a beautiful edifice, plush carpet, quiet and dimly lit, with only a quarter of the lighting turned on in the sanctuary. I took a seat down toward the front. Shortly, a thin well-dressed gentleman stood up from a handful of people. Minister Ben. He called everyone to attention as if they knew what to do. He gave honor to God and said we give honor to our overseer and pastor in their absence. He closed his eyes as he clenched his left fist and started to say softly, "Jesus, Jesus, Jeeesussss, Jesus," continuing with "We are calling on your name, Lord, but we know you are already here, because this is your house and you dwell in this house."

I noticed he wore a thick gold chain around his neck with a glittering gold cross attached. I could not help but notice as he stomped his left foot saying "Glory, glory, glory" how the gold cross moved from side to side, as it sometimes bounced around on his chest. As I refocused on what he was saying, I heard, "We come before Your presence to offer You thanks…" As the volume of his voice ratcheted up, he said, "I say thank you, Jesus. Thank you, Jeeesussss. Thank you, Lord of Host. King of kings, you have been better to me than I have been to myself and I thank ya…Yas–Sah…Yas–Sah…I thank you, Lord and Heavenly Father. Give Him some praise, y'all… Give Him what belongs to Him…Praise Him, he is the almighty God. Oh God…Doesn't sound like nobody in here but me, so I'm gonna praise Him myself if I have to."

Minister Ben asked everyone to get on their knees for prayer and to call on God like never before. He said, "I want you to pull on God until you have a breakthrough. Don't be quick to come up off your knees, spend time with God. Don't rush or hurry God."

After one and one half hours, Reverend Helen, who is a longtime member and trustee board member of the church, stood up to order everyone from their knees. She said, "Walk around, move around while you are praying." Reverend Helen was known best for telling parishioners in time of their troubles, "Don't worry, everything is going to be all right." The parishioners removed themselves from their knees, most were positioned in between rows of chairs, and they began to walk around the sanctuary. As they walked some spoke in tongues with their eyes barely open. People maneuvered around the sanctuary in and out of the aisles with their hands lifted—almost bumping into each other. As some walked in a trance hypnotic state, they moaned softly with repetitious, mum-mum-mum…I observed some parishioners lying at the altar moaning softly. I looked to the right and observed a few parishioners sitting shivering, and shaking, with their eyes shut.

My focus was distracted when Minister Ben took hold of the microphone, yelling loudly, "Ambush the devil. Ambush the devil… We gonna ambush the devil tonight. Somebody go back there and open those doors. Y'all tell the devil to get out. Get out, Devil." Minister Ben continued with, "I hate the devil, and he hates me, and the devil doesn't like y'all either." After that statement, he gave the parishioners a slight, tight smile. He told the parishioners they have to become radical like Jesus when they deal with the devil. Minister Ben directed the parishioners after this by saying, "Say amen, everybody." The parishioners responded to him by saying, "Amen."

Minister Ben says, "The devil doesn't like this church because we are righteous." I was not sure at this juncture by any stretch of my imagination to whom the devil might be by definition. This prayer meeting was charismatic, fiery, nontraditional, yet interesting to experience. If this was your first time attending this type of worship service, one or more thoughts would have most likely crossed your mind: (1) This is the church I want to belong to, (2) You are scared stiff, (3) How'd they do that? (4) Why can't my church be like this?

2

LOOKING BEHIND THE CROSS

WHO IS BEHIND YOUR CROSS? For some reason I have noticed more people wearing crosses. They come in a dizzying array of designs and shapes. A cross to me symbolizes spirituality, reverence, and Christianity. Perhaps crosses could mean different things to different people; it can be a symbol and source of power. Not long ago I was in church where I noticed bishops wearing remarkable and striking crosses. One bishop had his cross in his left shirt pocket. I was not sure if that was to keep the cross out of his way or if he wanted it closer to his heart. However, whether people wear a cross pinned to their clothing or from a chain around their neck, they are positioned behind the cross.

As Christ stumbled on His way to Mt. Golgotha, Christ carried the cross on His back. As He hung from the cross fading to His death, it remained behind Him. In essence Christ asserted Himself in front of the cross, whether carrying or hanging from it, the cross was firmly at His back. Not many people, if any, wear crosses hanging from their neck behind them.

In a business environment we use the phrase "getting out in front of situations" as the best way to handle and manage things. Taking control, doctors tell their patients, "We want to get out in front of this." Christ was in front of *and* in control of His crucifixion. When we leave this earthly life we are relieved from our cross.

The crucifixion of Christ was a mean-spirited event; however, the flip side of what happened on that day was for the greater good for all mankind. Of course, those events were the divine plan of God's grace. As we know, through the ages the cross has been symbolic of good and evil, mean-spiritedness, as well as love and kindness. Each individual wearing or carrying a cross represents what it symbolizes by their actions and behavior.

Christ's bearing and carrying the cross to Mt. Golgotha would not be the same as me carrying a cross to be crucified. My human nature would have been at best less humble. I don't know about other people, but I know I would have said something similar to *"Enough of this!"* among other choice words. This would have framed a different meaning to the crucifixion with us possibly still living in the Old Testament, if it were left up to me.

Most folks have a tendency to think in a paradigm—by thinking the cross is only a memorial that represents good. However, the human element allows the cross to take on different dynamics with shades of differentiated meanings and definitions—some positive, others negative.

Have you ever been uncertain when you see a person wearing a cross as to who is really behind the cross they are wearing? Our recent history is littered with stories that cause me to wonder.

Most of us remember Rev. Jim Jones who led a religious organization called the People's Temple. Reverend Jones became internationally notorious on November 18, 1978, when 918 people died at a settlement in Guyana and at a nearby airstrip in Georgetown Guyana's Capital. A total of 909 Temple members died in Jonestown, all but two from apparent cyanide poisoning, in an event termed "revolutionary suicide." Among them were over two hundred murdered children.

Also, David Koresh (born Vernon Wayne Howell). Koresh was the leader of a Branch Davidian religious sect. He believed he was the final prophet. Koresh died during a raid on April 19, 1993, by the US Bureau of Alcohol, Tobacco, Firearms and Explosives, the siege ended by the FBI with the burning of the Branch Davidian ranch. At the end of the siege, Koresh, fifty-four adults, and twenty-one children were dead.

Some might remember the fall of the Jim Baker Ministry, Evangelist Jimmy Swaggart Ministries, and the A. A. Allen Revivals Ministries. Reverend Allen died on June 11, 1970, at fifty-nine years of age. His autopsy reported his death as being directly related to acute alcoholism. Two of Reverend Allen's milestones were in the 1950s. He was one of the first ministers, along with Oral Roberts, to open his revival meetings to interracial crowds. In the mid-1950s he urged Pentecostal ministers to establish independent churches that would be freed of denominational control.

According to the *Biblical Recorder*, "September 27, 2009, David Treadway, a pastor, was found dead on Sunday morning in his car by his wife. The pastor had told his congregation several months earlier he was under doctor's care for depression. The church leadership stated their pastor had "succumbed to the disease of depression."

weCT-TV6 in North Carolina reported a federal jury has found Pastor Anthony Jinwright and his co-pastor wife, Harriet, guilty of tax evasion charges. Federal prosecutors accused them of failing from 2002 to 2007 to report $1.8 million of their $5 million income. They alleged that the Jinwrights used the money to fund their lavish lifestyles of fancy cars, homes, and trips even as their west Charlotte church struggled financially.

In 2008, Alabama pastor Anthony Hopkins was jailed after his deceased wife was found in a freezer. Evangelist Beverly Jackson of Inspirational Tabernacle Church of God in Christ in Jackson, Alabama, told CBS affiliate WKRG-TV that Pastor Hopkins had just preached about forgiveness Monday night when sheriff deputies placed him under arrest. According to Jackson, Hopkins told her that his wife died four years earlier while giving birth to their youngest son. Despite his pronouncements, Pastor Hopkins was found guilty of murder and is presently serving fifty-one years in prison.

In an online article posted August 16, 2011, "the police are investigating if drugs were involved in the death of a Florida megachurch pastor who was found dead in his Times Square hotel room. There was an envelope filled with white powder allegedly inside the shorts of the

Reverend Zachery Tims Jr., forty-two, the *New York News* reported. Tims led an eight-thousand-member church named New Destiny Christian Center."

I am sure all the aforementioned pastors and ministers had some contact or kinship with a cross—whether it was the cross they bear in their lives, a cross hanging someplace in their churches or home, or a cross worn on their person. There was a cross somewhere, someplace in each of those lives.

I was taught from my Bible studies that the Bible is God's mind.

> You come to the help of those who gladly do right, who remember your ways. But when we continued to sin against them, you were angry. How then can we be saved? All of us have become like one who is unclean, and all our righteous acts are like filthy rags; we all shrivel up like a leaf, and like the wind our sins sweep us away. No one calls on your name or strives to lay hold of you; for you have hidden your face from us and have given us over to our sins. (Isaiah 64:5–7 NIV)

In Romans 2:10–12 (KJV) we learn, "For there is no respect of persons with God." We all make mistakes. The Bible is filled with stories of redemption. I give due honor to leadership; however, I am able to face the fact that we all are apt to error with the potential to fall short on responsible standards.

What personality is behind *your* cross? Who is behind the cross of your pastor? Preaching an alluring sermon, singing, stomping your feet, clapping your hands, jumping, shouting, dancing around, having a sensational testimony, prospering, gifted, anointed are not a means to an end.

John 4:3–5 (KJV) tells us, "You are of God, little children, and have overcome them, because He who is in you is greater than he who is in the world."

I took the liberty to look up the word "cross" at dictionary. com. Take a look at some of the definitions:

1. A structure consisting essentially of an upright and a transverse piece, upon which persons were formerly put to death. The Cross is a symbol of Christianity. 2. Temporarily in an irritable or fretful state; unpleasant, unkind, and inclined to snarl or be spiteful. Synonyms: contradicts, cranky, ill-tempered, and testy.

What character is behind *your* cross? How did you represent your faith yesterday, today, or at this moment? Wearing a cross represents good or evil that is reflected by what you say and how you behave, demonstrating to the world perhaps how you believe and not so much how you feel. If one professes to be Christlike, their life is the only Bible some people will ever read. Remember, thoughts become words, words become actions, and actions become habits, shaping your character. Character becomes your destiny. The present will become history as the future will become the present.

LOOKING BEYOND THE CROSS

WHEN THE PEOPLE IN OUR lives are beloved, we are able to see beyond the cross they bear and crosses they put on. Self-proclaimed ministers, pastors, evangelists, prophets, politicians, kings, queens, priests, and celebrities are above reproach and impunity for misconduct if they are adored and beloved by people. The idea that accountability does not apply to ministers and the powerful is sometimes a reality. Most parishioners are convinced that their minister is incapable of any wrongdoings.

Evangelist Oral Roberts, according to the Christian Research Institute, alleged a revelation from God. Roberts claimed that unless he received $4.5 million for scholarships at Oral Roberts University Medical School, God would take him home. In other words, God was going to kill him if he didn't raise $4.5 million by a certain time.

In September 2004, WRAL news reported the arrest of Melvin Bynum, the pastor of Cry Out Loud Ministries in Sanford, North Carolina. Pastor Bynum pleaded guilty to voluntary manslaughter in connection with the strangulation death of forty-year-old Marnita, his wife of nineteen years. During the investigation, the parishioners were reluctant to cooperate with the police. After the pastor's arrest, the police made a statement informing the news that at the start of the investigation the members were not being very helpful, saying they were fearful of speaking out against the pastor and his ministry. One young lady said she was afraid of the pastor's adjutants, feeling intimidated by them. Direct and indirect intimidation and fear play a part in some ministries to tamp down criticism of misconduct of church leadership regimes. This is not uncommon for churches that have intimidating leadership regimes to be governed by strict legalistic rules and self-made doctrines.

Congregants are trained and brainwashed not to question or look beyond people who are self-proclaimed servants of God holding Bibles and wearing crosses. Parishioners in strong legalistic church organizations are forbidden to question the church leadership regime's motives or behaviors. Often these regimes will tell the parishioners not to question God, meaning everything they do is of God. More so, do what I say and never mind what I do. I feel compelled by my heart to inform those who want to acquire further perceptive: be aware of Bible-toting, cross-wearing folk saying they are called by God. If it sounds too good to be true, it probably is. Many parishioners cannot face the truth or did not think of being informed or educated on facts.

I have followed the Eddie Long case where Pastor Long was accused of having sexual relations with four young men. The church compensated them for two years, paying each $40,000 per year prior to them filing a lawsuit. The *Christian Post* reporter Elena Garcia wrote,

> Eddie Long Case Closed: Four Suits Officially Dismissed: The official status of the lawsuits, all filed in September 2010, is now "closed," according to the court's website." After a series of discussions, all parties involved have decided to resolve the civil cases out of court. "This decision was made to bring closure to this matter and to allow us to move forward with the plans God has for this ministry," stated Art Franklin. Three of the four suits against Long also listed New Birth Missionary Baptist Church and Long Fellows as defendants. The web site reddingnewsreview.com, reported Pastor Long paid $25 million to settle the

civil claims and also gave a private apology to the accusers. It was reported in October 2014, New Birth Missionary Church in North Carolina closed its doors; defaulting on over $10 million that placed the church into foreclosure.

We cannot judge Pastor Long. That remains for the day of Judgment. We can only deal with the merit of the facts. The case was closed before the final chapter, leaving us forever wondering why the accusers and Pastor Long settled out of court. Minister and Pastor Misconduct are on the rise, or at least are more apt to coming to the surface. In a survey of Southern Baptist Church pastors published in 1993 in the edition of the *Journal of Pastoral Care*, Jeff Seats revealed that 14.1 percent of ministers surveyed admitted to engagement in sexual behavior that was inappropriate for ministers.

Congregants should be aware of the inner workings of their church leadership regime. Rogue leaders will say or do whatever they want to their flocks under the cloak of "God said it and that settles it." How can you defend yourself with a church corporate leadership regime who checkmates you with "God said it and that settles it"? It can sometimes be a tough call as to who is saying what. This is what the Bible says, "Cursed is the one who trusts in man, who draws strength from mere flesh and whose heart turns away from the Lord" (Jeremiah 17:5 NIV). I personally know of people who appeared to be devout churchgoing Christians who have since died from the HIV virus (AIDS). As each death was connected to behaviors that challenged their church's teachings, the church corporate regimes tried to push these illnesses under the carpet. My mom who for over forty-five years has been the founder and pastor of her church said to me, "People can't handle certain information." However, the business side of me knows you only make an informed decision by having current, accurate information.

Pastors and ministers can preach grace but such little sense of their own need for it. They are frequently wrong, their conduct is imperfect, their leadership is lacking, and their best intentions often come up short. Once pastors and ministers believe that admission of error is a diminishment of their character and their capacity to lead, the clock to their demise starts running down. Whether from the pulpit, the boardroom, in correspondence or personal interaction, pastors and ministers must find the grace to continuously reach for the *mea culpa*. If you can't see it, accept it by faith and you will lengthen your tenure with God's people.

In March 2014, Bishop Bobby Davis of Miracle Faith World Outreach Church in Bridgeport, Connecticut, dropped dead in the face of his church congregation. This happened after being confronted by his wife and congregants about an affair he had in prior years. The ability to look beyond the failures of those who stand behind the pulpit preaching hell and condemnation while they themselves fail the basic standards of Christianity can be daunting. It takes a strong character not to place 100 percent of your confidence in that person. For this is the same person who can remove your state of well-being from you at his will. A standard principle I adopted in business and one used by President Ronald Reagan: "Trust, but verify."

My observation of folk in general is based on what they say and do as opposed to how they say they will behave. I have no jurisdiction or say over a person's relationship with their God, nor do I know if their soul is going to hell or heaven. I have, however, heard pastors call parishioners "dumb sheep" over the pulpit. This caused me to think, *Based on whose standard?* My belief has always been each of us has a personal relationship with our Maker. No one can take it or judge it away from us. My intellect does not fail me when it comes to the person speaking through the microphone as they hold up the Bible, wearing a cross and denouncing me as one of God's children. You can best be served by being aware of what hocus-pocus scare tactics and fear men can create. Be aware of preachers using Jesus as the boogeyman, as if Jesus is the villain who is going to get you if you don't do what he or she says. This is no more than folklore and a way for a preacher to appear empirical. Learning to look beyond the cross will give you a broader base on which unwavering redemption is found and grounded.

MY CHURCH FIRM

I HAVE NOTICED IN MY latter years that worshipers don't take the time to examine what ministers say or do. There is an extraordinary amount of misconception and nonfactual stories spread among churchgoers. Many don't take responsibility to detect what go on around them. Recently the *Washington Post* reported this headline: "Md. Church Where Senator is Minister Grapples with Debt." For the second time during his career as a minister, a church led by Maryland senator C. Anthony Muse has fallen into financial peril. The *Washington Post* further stated, "According to a filing with the State Ethics Commission, Muse owns three properties in addition to his home in Fort Washington: a vacation home in St. Inigoes, a rental property in Silver Spring, and an unimproved lot in Fort Washington. The church's bankruptcy filing also lists two debts, totaling nearly $1.2 million, to a mortgage company and a bank, and one of more than $250,000 to a Greenbelt law firm. An additional $66,000 is owed to a heating and air-conditioning company and more than $32,000 to a utility."

If you are in search of a church, count your time and seasons of looking, as a time of spiritual growth and discernment. Be thankful for friendly churches, but do not be overly impressed with superficial greetings. The real test of service is investing in each other's lives. There are many eloquent sermons and put-on theatrics in churches that gives one a tingly, warm, fuzzy feeling. Some teachings are therapeutic, motivational, and comforting, *but* does it really feed the sheep? If you are a Bible-believing, Word-eating Christian, this is what the book of John says:

> Again Jesus said, "Simon son of John, do you love me?" He answered, "Yes, Lord, you know that I love you." Jesus said, "Take care of my sheep." The third time he said to him, "Simon son of John, do you love me?" Peter was hurt because Jesus asked him the third time, "Do you love me?" He said, "Lord, you know all things; you know that I love you." Jesus said, "Feed my sheep." (John 21:16–18 NIV)

If you, like me, are not a theologian, I would only feel safe to say sheep are fed with scripture. Taking a text from the Bible, eloquently waxing over it, and raising a contemporary subject to the masses is somewhat diminutive. After studying and listening to hundreds upon hundreds of preachers, I have come to the realization that feeding sheep is a difficult and tedious task. Listening closely for years, I find that a grounded minister is one who can continually connect to an extended portion of a single passage of God's Word. The main point comes from within those scriptures, with supporting points, and the content is from those verses. I could very easily label some preachers as ministering by roaming. What I mean is, wandering in and out of the Bible. Going all over the place with whatever hits them at the moment.

These ministers never open their Bibles. Instead they direct people into interactive exercise regiments of constant "do this," "say that," "look over there," "look at your neighbor," "everybody on this side of the church move to that side of the church"—war dances, war crying, on and on. Often you will hear a roaming preacher say, "How did I get over here on this subject. This means God wants somebody in here to hear this." Or how about this one, "God just changed my message, I was going to preach on this, but I am now going to preach on that. God told me to change my message."

In some cases, are the masses really convinced that the preacher had a literal conversation with God? Maybe? It all depends on how convincing and confident the minister is with their audience. Why not just say, "I feel led in my heart to change my message today." A real crowd pleaser is when the minister says, "Everybody, hush, God is talking to me right now."

The things that I find in a sermon that strengthen the pastoral message and consistently feed God's sheep are fairly simple. They are the following:

1. A good sermon is a sermon I can follow.
2. The main point of the sermon is clear.
3. The sermon is well organized.
4. The preacher doesn't speak over my head.
5. The preacher doesn't repeat the same point over and over.
6. The preacher uses images, stories, and ways of speaking that afford me the opportunity to stay engaged to the message.
7. A strong sermon is rooted in the Bible.
8. A good sermon is not the opinion of the preacher; it's a word from God that has authority.
9. A good sermon deepens my faith.
10. A good sermon makes me a better person, a more loving person.
11. A sermon that doesn't call for and lead to transformation is only a noisy wagon or a loud minstrel show.

Good sermons call us to the cross and invite us into a new life in Christ. Preaching doesn't change people. God changes people through preaching. Churches must have good preaching. It is the primary trait and expectation of the pastor. Pastors in turn need to prepare their sermons through intense prayer and spiritual union.

I believe, moving forward, churches will become more progressive in the way we worship. Social and cultural trends are trending toward smaller intimate gatherings. Please understand. I am neither supporting nor projecting the closure of megachurches. However, megachurches should reform some of the things they do, similar to smaller church organizations, to hold on to their parishioners.

The new generation or what we call the Y generation of churches is more progressive, wanting to get their hands into the dirt of humanity to see real change in their communities and their lives. They will be free of the hype of events and more eager to dedicate themselves to something that requires sacrifice and results in biblical justice. They will come to the church brick-and-mortar buildings but will get disillusioned quickly if these events do not result in real opportunities to serve their world. Many church leadership regimes get you to feel that they are doing you a favor by accepting you as a member and allowing you to worship at their church organization. Look for a church that will provide you with opportunities to serve others. Try some small congregations. Pay attention to churches that are new or are meeting in interesting locations that you are not used to, like a park, hotel banquet room, or a warehouse, etc. Without me disparaging church corporate organizations, you might want to consider a few things and questions before you commit yourself and your family to a corporate church organization. Most importantly, arrive with the open heart of a guest and visitor to the church and not so much that of a movie critic.

1. What do we like about the church organization?
2. Will the pastor or leader allow you to interview them one-on-one?
3. Make a point to talk with the inner circle of people that are close to the pastor.
4. Find out from the pastor what their perspective is on you being a member of their organization.
5. Secure an interview with the trustee board members.

Have questions prepared (e.g., What percentage of church funds stay in the church, and what percentage of funds go into community or other programs?).

Professor *Devin A. Robinson* is a Pulitzer prize–winning newspaper columnist, social activist, author, and an economics professor at Oglethorpe University in Atlanta, Georgia, and the founder of Going Against the Grain Group. Professor Robinson—author of five books, speaker, and lecturer—says this about church funds:

> Like any other business, churches have utility bills and capital expenditures to pay. However, the uniqueness of a church is it is also a nonprofit, which means there are regulations to abide by in order to maintain its tax-exempt status. I recently asked my Facebook friends the following question: "Which is more important—the comfort of the pastor or the growth of the church?" Ironically, many felt the comfort of the pastor was more important. But here's the trick: a responsible nonprofit allocates at least 70 percent of its revenue toward the programs it was formed to develop. The other 30 percent would go toward administrative costs. The pastor's well-being should be in that 30 percent. Unfortunately, we catch a case of spiritual vertigo and slide the pastor's well-being into the 70 percent.

I have seen churches hide behind soup kitchens as their outreach ministry for years without any accountability. The other fund that flies indistinctly undetected is the building fund. Not to mention various programs in the community or around the globe they say are in operation but remain dysfunctional.

There are some ministers that are blessed with such large sums of money they no longer call it salary. They say publicly they don't take a salary but that they receive gifts from parishioners. The congregants are told they can claim their liberal giving as a write-off on their income tax. As a trustee board member responsible for church financial affairs, I found a small percentage of Christians overstating their contributions to the church; never understating their write-off for the tax year. At year's end some would argue with the trustee board that they gave more than what the record showed. I resolved this by giving congregants a monthly statement of what was on record with a year-to-date tally. What comes to my mind is how people tried to dump stuff they no longer wanted into the church because they could receive an easy write-off on their income tax.

During my tenure on the trustee board, I had a wealthy woman who was not a member donate a used table and eight chairs from her mansion in Chestnut Ridge, New York. Afterward she requested a write-off receipt from the church for $15,000. The woman refused to have her table appraised. My best guess was the table bought new was under $2,000. Needless to say, she was unhappy with me.

Church leadership regimes that have abundance in properties, lavish homes, luxury cars, jets, yachts, and other luxuries, including large sums of cash, will usually place these items under the church corporate name. This policy deters any scrutiny from the public or government officials. I often heard pastors and ministers refer to this scripture and passage during offertory time: "Give and it will be given to you. A good measure, pressed down, shaken together and running over, will be poured into your lap. For with the measure you use, it will be measured to you" (Luke 6:37–39, NIV). This scripture is a favorite among charismatic movements just before people march to the altar with their money in hand to drop it into a bucket. Some church leadership regimes have developed this passage into a song during the offering times for congregants as they line up in the aisles with their money. It really sets the mood backed by a B-3 Hammond organ. These church leaderships regimes have found the secret to cash flow. The concept I saw as a rule by leadership regimes was, Why take people's money when you can get them to offer it to you?

You may want to be aware of church leadership regimes' carefully crafted high-tech ponzi or pyramid schemes. A generic concept of the presentation is asking members to invest money with a high-yield rate on their investments. Churches often take out group death insurance policies on their members. The gist of the policy is the church pays the premium from tithe and offerings, and the beneficiary is the church corporate leadership regime and its pastor (CEO). The families in such policies usually have no entitlements or may not even be aware of the policies' existence.

Research the reputation of the church. Find out about the leadership and how they treat people and above all how they conduct themselves. Searching public records will allow you to seek out pending or past litigation involving the pastor and the church leadership regime. Check out if the Sunday school teacher or others have been incarcerated. Being incarcerated does not necessarily mean a person is a bad person. However, if there is a strong criminal element, you might put yourself on alert especially if the crime is of a sexual nature or involves children. If you are interested in donating your time and expertise to a particular church program, meet with the people who are involved with that area. You may want to find out if their educational programs are accredited and nonaccredited. Look to see if there is some type of succession plan, or is everything running helter-skelter, by seat of the pants, with ministers vying for the power chair. Are growth positions in the church organization authentic, or is it a game of tag, you are it? You will also want to know how a person is promoted in the organization. Find the undercurrents. The calm that appears on the surface may be the cover of the storms underneath.

Ask the trustee board for church corporate doctrines and rules. If you ask direct questions of the pastor, or other seemingly leaders and get indirect answers filled with epithets, and non transparent answers, become leery. Don't forget to ask about church business meetings, and how transparent the church corporation is to congregants.

Ensure for yourself that the pastor is spiritually and mentally sound and capable of helping you look after your spiritual well-being. There are churches where pastors have quietly glided into a state of narcissism. The narcissism and self-serving of pastors usually originate from flocks worshipping their pastor rather than respecting the pastor and worshipping God. Before you join you will want to understand exactly what is expected of your membership responsibilities, financial obligations, and physical attendance. Observe how members and folk close to the pastor behave; steering away from churches that appear to have lost their moral compass. I could go on with more, and certainly you can create a list of checkpoints of your own.

Often members join church corporations based on a feel-good moment, riding on their emotions and hype. Churches hungry for membership don't give you a chance to come down from the moments of manufactured mass-hysteria and ramped-up worship services. I strongly suggest that you take the time to do your homework. Be careful of churches that are run by whimsical spirituality guidelines. While we believe in allowing the spirit to have its way, do not be overly concerned when a man or woman stands up and says we can't control all things in a God-spirit-filled service.

Be more alert and attentive when people say "Everything is done when the spirit tells us to do it." For example, "We don't know when we will end the service or start the service. The services are run by the Holy Ghost." These bells and whistles could be the signs of the times. Their God is out of control when he shows up and shows out.

I want to hear my minister say "I feel in my heart" or "I feel led to say this or led to do this." A minister claiming and blaming God for every move he makes and does with "God told me to do this and that" might be showing the characteristics of a narcissistic leader. I cannot say it enough. Please check out what the ministry is about before you join.

I heard a pastor stand up and tell the congregation if a person comes three times in a row, they are considered a member of his church. I went down the road to a different church in the same town. There the pastor stood up and said if you are absent three Sundays from church, you are not considered a member of this church any longer.

Here is a quick reference scripture: "Furthermore, just as they did not think it worthwhile to retain the knowledge of God, so God gave them over to a depraved mind, so that they do what ought not to be done" (Romans 1:28 NIV).

A *reprobate mind* is a term used in the religious sector to describe a person who has been rejected by God. They have chosen to disregard the will of God. Because they refuse to walk a righteous life, God rejects them. God no longer extends His grace but turns them over to their lustful desires. Organizations, like people, can make decisions that are off-the-wall and irrational, making no sense other than to themselves.

Joining a church corporate organization is likened to a marriage. You will do the work before, during, or after, but you will do the work. Doing the homework on a church before you join will keep you from feeling you made a poor decision, or having buyer's remorse. Keep in mind, there is no perfect church or pastor.

However, you want to look for a progressive church organization that will help serve your purpose in life. There is nothing like having disappointments, so don't set yourself up for failed church relationships over and over again.

An interesting side note: During the Citizens United court case (a nonprofit organization), Justice Stephens said, "Although they make enormous contributions to our society, corporations aren't actually members of it. Corporations have no conscience, no beliefs, no feelings, no thoughts, no desires. They are not themselves members of we the people by whom and for whom our constitution was established."

You may be asking yourself why in the world a church would want to be incorporated. When you take the robes off the choir, the preacher leaves the pulpit, the lights are turned off, and the front door is locked—churches are businesses, corporations with bills to pay. Money is exchanged and sometimes laundered to sustain their power of existence.

On March 11, 2014, it was reported that the Lakewood Church in Houston was missing an estimated $600,000 from the church's safe. It has been reported since 2011 that church fraud is rising at the rate of 5.9 percent annually among Christian circles.

Without trying to appeal to your greater sense of corporate good, corporations are not evil—they are just profit-making machines. Sure, people start churches because it is a lucrative business. Folks who start churches without the compelling spirit of God calling for them to do so can be closely compared to politicians with the gift of rhetoric.

Most churches are incorporated and are listed as tax-exempt nonprofit organizations. Right now, some corporations are not very people friendly in corporate America. In all fairness, churches are almost forced to incorporate in order to be protected from personal liability from civil lawsuits.

Not long ago a husband and wife sued a minister over their young son's death. The minister proclaimed that God said the child was healed from a life-threatening disease. Sometime later the young lad died from the disease the healer said he was healed from. The parents were heartbroken. The parents sued and won their case.

The Atlanta Journal-Constitution reported two lawsuits filed against a church for molestation on May 23, 2012, in Clayton County State Court. Parents whose sons allegedly were molested by a volunteer at North Star Church in Kennesaw filed separate lawsuits against the church. The suits are pending.

We make choices on how we want to worship or what kind of church organization and leadership regime we trust with our beliefs and lives. Here are some information to enlighten the understanding of your church experiences and treatment by others.

In his book *Recovering From Churches That Abuse,* Dr. Ronald Enroth says,

> In an abusive church, the use of guilt and intimidation to control members is likely to produce members who have a low self-image who feel beaten down by legalisms, who have been taught that asserting oneself is not spiritual. One of the first disturbing characteristics to be reported by relatives, friends of members of these churches is noticeable change in personality, usually in a negative direction. Nearly all unhealthy churches attempt to minimize commitment to families, especially parents. Young people may be told that they now have a new spiritual family, complete with leaders that will re-parent them. Church loyalty is seen as paramount, and family commitments are discouraged or viewed as impediments to spiritual advancement. Control-oriented leaders attempt to dictate what members think, although the process is so spiritualized that members don't realize what is going on. A pastor or leader is viewed as God's mouth piece and in varying degrees a member's decision making and ability to think for oneself are swallowed up by the group. Pressure to conform and low tolerance for questioning make it difficult to be discerning.

A legalistic emphasis on keeping rules and a focus on the need to stay in prescribed boundaries is always present in unhealthy spiritual environments. The rigid lifestyle in these types of groups increase members' guilt feelings and contributes to spiritual bondage. This rigidity is often coupled with an emphasis on beliefs that would not receive great attention in mainstream evangelicalism.

In intense legalistic churches and organizations, the official public proclamations usually place special value on high moral standards. In some instances, there is a double standard for those in leadership and those in rank and file membership. For example abusive churches tend to have incidents of sexual misconduct more often than conventional churches; leaders sometime exhibit an obsessive interest in sexuality.

Authoritarian pastors are usually threatened by any outside expression of diverse opinions, whether inside or outside the group. When outside preachers are given access to the pulpit, they are carefully selected to minimize any threat to the leadership agenda. Coercive pastors are fiercely independent and do not function well in a structure of accountability. For the sake of public relations, they may boast they are accountable to a board of some sort, when actually the board is composed of "yes-men" who do not question the leader's authority.

Another hallmark of an authoritarian church is its intolerance of any belief system different from its own. They tend to measure and evaluate all forms of Christian spirituality according to their own carefully prescribed system, adopting an "us versus them" mentality.

A cardinal rule of abusive systems is "don't ask questions and don't make waves." A healthy pastor welcomes even tough questions. In an unhealthy church disagreement with the pastor is considered disloyalty and is tantamount to disobeying God.

People who repeatedly question the system are labeled rebellious, or disharmonious to the body of Christ. Persistent questions may face sanctions of some kind such as being publicly ridiculed, shunned, shamed, humiliated, or disfellowshiped.

Whether they admit it or not, abusive churches tend to view themselves as spiritually superior to other Christian groups. This religious elitism allows little room for outside influences. There can be no compromise with external sources, who, the leadership will say, really don't understand what is going on in the ministry anyway. Sometimes abusive groups illustrate a split level religion. There is one level for the public presentation and another for the inner circle of membership. The former is a carefully crafted public relations effort, the latter a reality level experienced only by the true believers.

Recruitment tactics are intense, even if they are not deceptive or fraudulent they can be manipulative or exploitive. Sometime high pressure religious groups are evasive about their true identity: We really don't have a name we are just Christians. A healthy Christian group should have no qualms about revealing who they are and what are their intensions. First impressions are not always correct. Sustained contact with an unhealthy church however, will usually reveal a pattern that is consistent with the characteristics we have identified. Members will be requested to serve, to become involved, to sign up for a variety of activities that, upon closer inspection, appear to maintain the system and serve the needs of the leadership.

> Abusive churches thrive on creative tactics that promote dependency. Emphasizing obedience and submission to leaders, these churches require a level of service that is overwhelming to its members, resulting in emotional turmoil and spiritual breakdowns.

If you find yourself in an abusive church relationship, don't be afraid to leave. Get up, walk out, and don't look back. Pray, get council and therapy if you need it. Just leave—mad, hurt, angry, happy. Leave the unhealthy toxic environment. It is a hazard to you and your family's health and mental attitude. Go!

A parishioner informed me of how a former Sunday school superintendent beckoned his family to rise to their feet while he gathered his belongings during a Sunday morning sermon. He walked with his family in tow down the center aisle and out the double doors. The congregants were mummified as they looked on with their mouths open. After you leave, don't go back expecting the church has changed, or expecting it will be different this time around. Once a church that abuses tells you who they are, believe them. Only go back if the leadership regime has changed, or they hang out a sign that says Under New Management or Under New Pastoral Care. Anything along those lines might allow you a favorable chance of survival.

I have seen people stay in churches that abuse because they think they can change it or they want to be a thorn in their side and fight with them. People get drawn into this magnetic field of dissonance trying to win some spiritual battle that results in placing them in a poor light. The leadership regime will isolate and ridicule the person and, in many cases, dress them down in front of the congregation. This tactic of public humiliation and embarrassment is used to scare congregants into line. Throughout this text I will refer to my mother's church as the Tabernacle Church. At the Tabernacle Church if you got out of alignment with the leadership regime and my mother's doctrines, you would be lambasted over the pulpit through a high-intensity cordless microphone. Mom's voice was projected through high-amperage speakers and subwoofers.

Through the tyranny of this culture, the congregants feared the moment if and when the lambasting happened to them. The rest of the congregation would watch their brother or sister being humiliated and dressed down while softly saying in a condescending tone, "Amen, Pastor, that's right, it's the truth." He who holds the microphone is in charge of the group.

Churches that abuse have done this for years. They know how, when, and what to do. If you experience church abuse from an organization, they will most likely not change. There is no reason for the leadership to change something that they feel is working for them. However, when you feel safer on the outside of these circles, something is a mite wrong. Many churches are in trouble because they have set themselves apart, symbolizing sanctity and holiness. But within those sacred, or for a better word, *secret* circles, a gambit of things are going on. Within those walls there is drug use, alcohol abuse, theft, fighting, backstabbing, cutthroat behavior, tax evasion, child abuse, inappropriate sexual behavior, vindictiveness, lying, cheating, adultery, idol worship, infidelity, anti-trust violations, murder, vain worship, and the list goes on. For criminal activity and offensive inappropriate behaviors to be eliminated, we must look to the congregants and leadership regimes to do the right thing inside the church body. A church loses its effectiveness to attend to God's flocks, souls, and communities when high levels of variable offensive activity are taking place.

I have often wondered if churches have been hijacked by leadership regimes. It appears that some leadership regimes have no accountability to themselves, their God, or anyone else. Stay in an abusive church if you choose to be there. I bid you Godspeed if you are in search of a church. Please take your time.

LEGALISM VS. LEGALISM

REALLY, WHAT IS *LEGALISM*? *LEGALISM* is the strict adherence or the principle of strict adherence to law or prescription. Think of it as the letter of the law rather than the spirit. In theology, legalism is the doctrine that salvation is gained only through good works. All conduct is judged in terms of adherence to precise law with strict legal control over all activities. With it comes a system of rewards, punishments, and absolute monarchy.

The impact of legalism is horrendous. It causes churches to fall out over worship services. It makes generations distrust each other. It causes Christians to judge one another. It makes us superficial. It makes us hypocrites. How many churches still argue over music? How many churches fight over small, mundane things?

Legalism positions churches into competition with each other. I have visited cities, towns, and villages where churches are not just on the same street but literally positioned in storefronts next door to each other. In business, when a company places itself on the same street or in some instances next door to a competitor, it is clear they are moving in on the market, drawing a line in the sand.

Legalism puts churches into squabbling packs of protectors who are more interested in their own interests, rights, and membership to a low-cost country club. It keeps churches from innovating as they enforce "the way it's always been." Legalism has two results: (1) preoccupying Christians with intramural warfare, and (2) barricading the doors to lost people and the under-churched.

Doing interviews for this book, it was most refreshing to speak with someone who was not intimidated or apathetical about speaking their heart and mind. Take a look at one woman's view of her church relationship:

> Depending on the church. Churches are led by people who possess all the frailties we all possess and therefore are all imperfect. I don't consider every word uttered from the mouth of a preacher to be sacrosanct. Those who require a role model to guide their lives are greatly influenced, and those who require less guidance from outside themselves are less predisposed. However, it is a great social medium at least for me.

I am reminded of a woman who became disenchanted with mom's ministry, church rules, and the dysfunction of the leadership regime. Driven by her discontent and zeal, she started a church in Mount Vernon, New York. The building was cited to be condemned by the city building inspectors. She covertly operated in this abandoned building, placing a small number of parishioners in harm's way. I call them squatters, or for lack of better words, the homeless church. This went on for about one year before the illegal church was padlocked and sealed by the city of Mount Vernon.

What triggered the building being sealed off were the following events: The assistant pastor had an argument with his wife over pornography she found in his cell phone. The wife brought the cell phone to the pastor to show her the pornography. The pastor made the decision to silence and suspend the assistant pastor's duties for a period of time. The assistant pastor was not in accord with the discipline procedure so angrily called the city building and codes compliance department, who then ousted the squatting church by sealing the building off. Then there is the story of Minister Shame, a popular minister at the Tabernacle Church, who misplaced his cell phone in the church one day. Now one of his weaknesses was womanizing. Minister Shame practiced luring women into his bed with the pretense of marriage to follow. Usually the end result of his wolflike tendencies devastated these young women. Deceived by Shame, they would ultimately depart from the church; however, not until after buying him expensive or lavish gifts.

That cell phone Minister Shame lost, well, it was discovered by another minister not fond of Minister Shame. The minister who found the phone breached privacy and viewed stored pictures of naked women. I verified this with my mother, who told me it was true. After learning of the naked pictures, my mother evoked a rule that called for Shame's silence, sitting him down from any church activities.

I particularly remember one of mom's secretaries who got caught up in Minister Shame's web of deception. After the relationship stalled, Mom met with the secretary and Minister Shame, where the secretary admitted they were having consensual sex.

Minister Shame, on the other hand, denied having sex with the young woman, manipulating mom into believing the secretary was a liar. Before the meeting ended, mom's secretary got up from her chair and stomped out, never to be seen or heard from again. Mom told me she did not know where she went. She just disappeared.

Often, mom would say how she wished Minister Shame would leave her church. "I just let him sit here and ignore him. He is always starting something. If his father was not an elder here, I would have thrown his butt out. I know his momma don't like me either."

After Minister Shame's tarnished reputation, his father, the elder, stood up on a Sunday morning telling the few congregants, "I am tired of y'all picking on my son."

In early 2012 Shame's father left the Tabernacle Church after forty-two years. This came on the heels of his son's discord with the leadership. As justification to her dwindling congregation, mom used the same ole play book: "He ain't nobody, they can all leave." She continued, "Anybody else feels like they want to leave? God told me that there are some more of you that are not with me, and God is going to weed you out!" Mom ended by telling her congregants that the elder was not saved and his Christianity and loyalty was always in question.

A few months later the elder's son started his own church not far from the Tabernacle Church. Shame departed the Tabernacle after being accused of allegedly groping a female member during a church service. Mom said, "We should have called the police and had him arrested." Mom went on to say, "Millie could have had him arrested, you know."

Shame was ordained by a self-proclaimed apostle from Atlanta, Georgia. The apostle had become one of mother's favorite preachers visiting her church and preaching often. She would publicly call him her son until he ordained Shame to pastoral care of a church without informing her. Only then did mom sound the alarm, warning congregants to be watchful as to whom they let pray for them. She told the congregants they might want to check people's cell phones to see what they have in them before being allowed to put hands on their foreheads to pray for them.

In the case of mom's secretary, Tabernacle Church was run with an ironclad fist while Minister Shame just wandered off doing as he pleased. Like Las Vegas, "What happens in the Tabernacle stays in the Tabernacle."

The inner circle ministers, the church leadership regime, gained my mother's favoritism and trust by placing her on a pedestal of "does no wrong, you have no fault." They supported her through praise for her work, gifts, and money. The inner circle led my mother, the pastor, to believe she was the most anointed pastor in the world. They were responsible for branding her with being closer to God than anyone on earth, even leading her to believe she was a perfect woman in God's eyes. The inner circle was the core for feeding my mother's misguidance.

Mom was never challenged for any reason. In life a pancake has two sides, but in the Tabernacle Church it was always a one-sided story. If something happened, the inner circle knew to always give mom the victim chair. It's everyone vs. the pastor. I have a growing fear for pastors and ministers. Ministers should unburden people—challenge them, not burden them. In describing what the Pharisees teachings did to the people, Jesus said, "They tie up heavy, cumbersome loads and put them on other people's shoulders, but they themselves are not willing to lift a finger to move them" (Matthew 23:4 NIV). When we read this, we assume the Pharisees had bad motives. But when we study their history, their motives were actually good. What they did by creating all of those infamous rules was to make the Old Testament law applicable to people's lives. They'd read "Keep the Sabbath holy," and out of concern that everyone could actually do it, they'd create rules like items used for work can't be touched on the Sabbath, you shouldn't take more than five hundred steps on the Sabbath, etc.

Their motivation was to help through defining what people could do. However, in their desire to make the Bible applicable, they actually created burdens that weighed their people down. For example, a minister might speak on faith then give parishioners a bunch of steps to attaining it. Without realizing it, ministers actually burdened people who were already carrying a heavy load. People should be given practical applications. Ministers should be careful to unburden their flock. For example, emulating Jesus, "My yoke is easy and my burden is light." Simplify rather than complicate. Look to what God and all He has done, not just at people and all that they need to do.

I can recall being told about a lady who arrived for service at the Tabernacle Church and was turned away at the double doors to the sanctuary. The usher told her that her blouse sleeves were too short to come in. When she complained about the situation of how she was treated, the church leadership regime told her the usher was right by making her go away from the church. To my understanding she never returned to the church, being infuriated and hurt.

Another stricter definition of *legalism* from the *Oxford English Dictionary*: "The principles of those who hold a theological position of adhering to the law as opposed to the Gospel; the doctrine of justification by Works, or teaching which savors of that doctrine." Legalism is, at best, a plan that tries to blind and disrupt God's plan for grace. It is a system that teaches that a person can do something to earn merit, salvation, or blessings from God. As in any work-based merit system, with legalism a person trie41s to please God, assist God, or glorify God by human power. This leads me to this scripture: "Then we will no longer be infants, tossed back and forth by the waves, and blown here and there by every wind of teaching and by the cunning and craftiness of people in their deceitful scheming" (Ephesians 4:14 NIV).

Religion is a system where man through his own efforts tries to earn the approval of God. Most religions are legalistic. "And if by grace, then it cannot be based on works; if it were, grace would no longer be grace" (Romans 11:6 NIV).

Understand, religious legalists are convinced that God works by the same system as the human system of work and rewards, the way of commerce and free enterprise. For example, I work for you and you pay me. I work for God, and God rewards me by saving me and giving me blessings. God has no need or desire for our works. Our work is actually an offense to God. "All of us have become like one who is unclean, and all our righteous acts are like filthy rags; we all shrivel up like a leaf, and like the wind our sins sweep us away" (Isaiah 64:6 NIV).

It is not legalism to have high standards; it is legalism to try to impose those standards on others as a pathway to spirituality. The work that has already been done by Christ on the cross gives God the go-ahead to do for mankind. Grace means that man has received from God that which he hasn't earned or deserved. Nothing we are, or nothing we can do, is enough to qualify us for anything the Lord has to give us. Actually, our works cause us to be arrogant in the presence of God. Our ego urges us to emphasize our role in what God has done.

Churches mix legalism into salvation. For example, belief is not making a public spectacle of yourself, displaying or having great sorrow or a show of tears. Believe is not joining the church membership. The Gospel states Believe needs nothing! Legalism makes a people-centered church. Grace makes a God-centered church that loves people. Pentecostal churches, such as where I was brought up, using Christianity as its base laced with extreme legalism, looks like this: thinking one is spiritual because he doesn't do certain things or follows a certain do's and don'ts list. Living the Christian life is conformity in dress, mannerisms, and speech. Your sins are worse than mine; therefore, I am more spiritual. You are carnal and less spiritual than I. If you don't agree with me, you are self-righteous. You have to protect a person who has a perversion to child molestation or other unacceptable societal ills of misconduct because he belongs to the body of Christ. Worship behavior includes speaking in tongues, groaning, dramatizing being in a trance, fainting, rolling around on the ground, etc.

Bond to rituals—the idea that one is spiritual because they go through a variety of ceremonies. In the apostles' day, the Jews promoted circumcision as a necessary ritual to be a Christian. These days, baptism is used, or one of the other sacraments. The concept is that one is spiritual if you are faithful in praying, giving, witnessing, attending church, etc. These are legitimate activities of Christian growth and the filling of the Holy Spirit. Extreme self-sacrifice, extreme self-denial, and giving up of necessities are sometimes believed to impress God. God's ways are far different from our own.

In many situations the Bible is misinterpreted, and these rules become reality to the members. Take the doctrine of baptism. Legalism makes it the mandate for church membership. Man-made rules and doctrines of church leadership regimes can become no less than modern-day Pharisees, eventually driving people away from Christianity. Misguided religions try to impose political beliefs that are somewhat narrow-minded.

Legalism is a process of turning away from the truth. Once legalism starts to operate in a believer's life, they become suspicious of others' motives, methods, and message. Hard-line suspicions can break down a person's mind. Some individuals exposed to influential legalism become damaged both spiritually and emotionally, falling away from Christianity, or they have deep emotional scars that have caused depression.

LEGALISM AND LEADERSHIP

LEGALISM IS OFTEN SEEN IN leadership before it is seen in the congregation. It takes the doctrine of separation and makes it spirituality, getting others to rally around the division and separations of others. An example is when members of a church are told to shun former members by not speaking or associating with them. Unsaved people can smell legalism. Maybe not in all cases are they able to understand it or explain it. It may take a while to sniff it out, but they'll find it. When they do, they'll run for the door. A legalistic person has been *bewitched*. This term means evil brought upon you by vain praise. A person wrapped up in legalism is described as foolish, meaning not understanding.

Legalism is a robber of Christian benefits. It robs people of their understanding of the Word of God and all of the benefits of the grace of God. A legalist person does not learn from experience. They have great tenacity despite failures and vain strivings. They can't see the error of their ways. Legalists are never satisfied and never in step with satisfying others. Easier said, they are troublemakers. Grace is the only system that does not magnify the deficiencies of believers. If I were able to sum up legalism into one word, it would be *no!*

Here are a few examples of legalistic doctrines and church policies: Can I go see a Broadway Show? – "No!" Can I wear this color? – "No!" Can my children play sports? – "No!"

Can I buy a wide screen television for my home? – "Yeah… but! no!"

The freedom to express oneself is not tolerated, even certain forms of Christian music become wrong. Musicians are stifled and not allowed to use their God-given talents, adhering only to church-approved music. Freedom to have one's own identity is limited. Individuals are treated as robots that must be programmed. The programming includes guilt and coercion. Once a person feels the guilt of their actions, they open up, becoming publicly honest about themselves. Sometimes unscrupulous preachers move in, taking advantage of the unsuspecting parishioner. The preacher will use the congregant's undying honesty to import them back into guilt.

I have seen congregants so guilt stricken to the point that they end up being of no help to anyone. God has forgiven them, but they need to be told by their pastor to forgive themselves. Instead they spend their lives in prayer lines, attending church service after service and giving their entire paychecks to the church leadership regime. Never ridding themselves of the complexity of their guilt issues, this person usually does not develop out of these cycles of cleansing rituals and into God's grace principles. It becomes the gift that keeps on giving for some preachers.

Eventually this parishioner becomes codependent on the leadership regime rather than feeling an aspiration for fellowship. This is often seen with parishioners who are easily confused and appear challenged in thinking for themselves. Folks with a history of being easily intimidated and persuaded by terminology become prime targets for being taken advantage of by church corporate leadership regimes.

When a person is ridiculed for asking questions, it starts a downward spiral to being dumbed down and apathetical toward church leadership regimes. I had a preacher say to me once, "You ask too many questions, you think too much. Stop thinking so much." This in itself can cause low self-esteem, forcing members to submit to church-imposed doctrines. Individuals that do not adhere to the guidelines are sometimes shunned or, worse yet, told they are living in sin and must get right with God. In reality, they are being told that they must get right with the church-imposed rules and guidelines. I believe continuous exposure to giving another person control over your mind and well-being weakens you. A person in this situation could become susceptible to moral misconduct, causing reason and sensibility to become detached. Secrecy within the church becomes another tool. Some of the stricter churches use secrecy to maintain a strong control over their congregants. Secrecy sets an environment of who belongs and who does not belong in our circle.

Legalistic folks take on a behavior where they form their own conclusion to matters without the facts. They call this the gift of discernment. I have seen their discernment in operation in many situations where they were just absolutely wrong. God-given common sense would have ruled out better, if there is such a thing as common sense.

I am reminded of a deacon in mom's church. Deacon Bob Thomas. Bob stood about six feet four inches tall, a grizzly-looking man. He was scary from the sense he looked like the character Lurch from the television show "The Addams Family." He served on the usher board and had a look that he would hurt you physically before you could bat an eye. He was stern and serious, and most of the small children were afraid of him, thinking he was mean. Deacon Thomas was a person you steered away from. You kind of got the impression he was not the man to have a confrontation with, unless you had a stick in your hand, or some other weapon.

Whenever mom gave him directions or orders, Deacon Thomas took everything literally. He publicly advocated following the church rules stringently, except when it came to himself. I was not surprised to hear in later years that he was abusive to his wife, who was a minister at the church.

One Sunday I was playing the organ during the devotional service when I notice Mr. Luke had entered the church. His wife was a devout follower and member of the church, serving as one of the pastor's aides. She was a wonderful lady. Like her, Mr. Luke was a nice person, even though he was a functioning alcoholic. Mr. Luke was a small, framed, slim man, and my best guess, he looked to be well underweight. A tailor by profession, he was articulate, using appropriate and proper English. Speaking to him you got the impression he was well educated. On this particular Sunday it was apparent Mr. Luke had been drinking before his arrival to church.

Deacon Thomas was at the door that Sunday, and he and Mr. Luke had a history of going back to other church arguments. He stopped Mr. Luke and held him at the door inside the church. It appeared that both men were arguing about something, which soon escalated into a physical struggle in the rear of the church.

Before anyone could intervene, Deacon Thomas had grabbed Mr. Luke up off the ground and threw him down four feet away from where the struggle was taking place. Mr. Luke landed on his back, stretched out stiff. When he hit the ground, we heard glass shatter. He had a fifth of liquor in his back pocket. By this time other men were at the scene in the rear of the church managing the ruckus as mom hurriedly went there to find Mr. Luke struggling to stand up. As he got his footing, crying and shaking his left index finger at Deacon Thomas, he looks at mom and eloquently intoned in a deliberate voice, "Pastor, someday I am going to kill that man."

You see, Deacon Thomas was a great model for a bouncer, scaring people into behaving properly. Through his own behavior, influenced by church rules, he decided that Mr. Luke could not enter the church for any reason, under any circumstance. That led to the physical confrontation inside the church doors, which was frightful for smaller children. Plus, I am not so sure I would like Deacon Thomas to have the first contact with any visitor or member in any setting, let alone be the church greeter. He was a person that needed to be introduced to interpersonal skills training courses.

Years later, the church had an usher that walked around like she was a prison guard. She was not friendly, bringing attention to herself by bothering people for no apparent reason. The members called her the Warden. During one service she asked a lady holding her baby to stop gently rocking her child because "I have been instructed to take care of the church chairs." Now the church chairs were manufactured in Atlanta, Georgia, by a company called Church Chairs. The chair frames were made of tubular steel.

The same usher would bodily block parishioners from leaving the sanctuary during the offertory, prayer, or preaching times. I remember a lady escorting her small daughter to the lavatory and was stopped at the double doors. The woman was awfully upset after her child wet herself. This usher actually imprisoned people in the sanctuary by enforcing the leadership rules and doctrines. Mom would express that we need tough folk like that ushering "because these church people will tear up your church if you let 'em." After hearing this, all I could do was shake my head from side to side.

Here is another story that is a sign of our times, where the Tabernacle Church was challenged by the new electronic age. A young man and his wife were attending a Sunday morning service. He had a handheld wireless device with the Bible programmed into it. When the minister asked everyone to open their Bibles to a specific book, chapter, and verse, the husband used his wireless device. As the gentleman was navigating to the referenced scripture, a male usher observed the handheld device. From the outer aisle he abruptly called to the man, "Cell phones are not allowed, you have to turn that off and put it away." The usher was caught in a paradigm, not understanding that the visitor was reading the scripture from a handheld device. The irony being the usher only recognized the Bible as a book with the inscription "Holy Bible" on the cover.

Some churches use fear as a method to obtain members. A typical tactic would be to word sermons like this: "What if you walk out this door and die. You may never get salvation and you will burn in hell forever." Or there's guilt: the preacher makes you feel unworthy to be in the presence of God as you have done wrong all your life. You need the inner circle to pray over you to circumvent being cursed and going to hell.

The voice of legalism comes with no real observation or discernment; it is shoot first, ask questions later. It does not allow you to think outside of the box. You are caught in a paradigm. My suggestion: when you see extreme legalism in a church, run for your life.

Here is an interview I did with an organist that left the Tabernacle Church corporate leadership regime. You may be able to identify with this story.

> After forty-years plus of this mental and verbal abuse,
> I made my decision. My first encounter with the

verbal abuse was when I first started going to the now Tabernacle Church Incorporated. The pastor stopped by the house one day and told my mother that I rolled my eyes at her. I was only…nine years old. I couldn't imagine someone saying that about me in those days. This modeled abuse continued during my tenure.

I recall another time. We were at LaGuardia airport in New York on our way to Chicago when the pastor said I was an embarrassment to her because she didn't like what I was wearing. All the while I was the one being embarrassed. She never came to my defense at any time like she did with others. Nothing that I did was ever good enough. One day during a call to take me to task on another matter, Pastor said, "Your family has always tried to take over my church." She talked about my mother, uncle, brother, friend, and my daughter, and then she went hard in on me. Telling me I was a liar, a hypocrite, and I was not a Christian, among other convoluted allegations. My response to her was that "she would never have to worry about me again. I will type up my resignation letter and send it to the church."

After I left, I stopped in on the church one Sunday to visit. This was after I bought my first home. The pastor stood up in the pulpit before her sermon and said to the congregation, "You think you're something because you bought a house, well, there's some more single women in here that God is going to bless with a house." But after that statement, I decided to just leave because I came to get a blessing and I didn't want to hear the abuse anymore. I never understood why she never cared for me. I tried many times to reach out and embrace my pastor, but in return my self-respect was marred, degraded, and demeaned, no matter my approach.

This interview, among many, is the reason I am writing to brothers and sisters in Christ who have walked from church doors with broken hearts. If your church attendance should fall off due to hurt and pain, then your church leadership regime infamously identifies a broken heart as a backslider. I have witnessed the pain and felt the disappointment.

In the case of the organist, her real trouble started when her sister married Minister Lesley. The organist, from her own observation and talking with her sister, made the first allegation toward Les's sexual preference to men. Les denied the allegations, and the war was on against the organist. He used the pastor to his advantage by telling falsehoods against her. This triggered the pastor to take on a more negative attitude and outlook toward the organist's future in the church. Earlier in the game, it appeared that mom had to make a decision as to who was worth more to her. Was it Minister Lesley or the organist?

Les was a uniquely talented individual. He had joined the Tabernacle Church when he was thirteen years old. Minister Lesley was this man-child who I call mom Version 2.0. By playing cozy and feeding mom's ego, he became a favorite. To ingratiate himself to her, he sometimes would eat food scraps from her plate. Plopping himself down next to her while sucking on a meatless steak bone and sipping from her almost-empty cup or glass, Les would tell the onlookers and table guests he would be blessed and more anointed by his unique ritual. This flattered mom to pieces. It was a real crowd pleaser.

Most people attending the Tabernacle Church and in the community had a sense that Minister Les preferred a same-sex partner. The church, though, had a stiff rule about gays: if you were gay, you were bound for hell. In this instance, the church leadership regime failed, as it denied Lesley to be who he truly was. Les's skeletons were hidden in the closet. Funny thing, skeletons don't like closets. If you spoke directly to Les's covert sexual behavior, you were doomed, and your demise was imminent. It would only be a matter of time.

You see, Les was an intricate piece to the leadership regime at the Tabernacle Church and he had a strong influence on mom. She believed whatever he said. Les was talented and could usually fit into wherever mom needed him. His answers to her were absolute and respectful: "Yes, ma'am" or "No, ma'am." When Les wanted to throw a person under the bus, using a very conventional approach, he would often manipulate mom into thinking negatively of people he did not like. In arranged clandestine meetings with her, I would hear him say, "Mom, I don't want to tell you what to do, but," and then he would go forward with whatever he was trying to get her to do. Later years, mom stopped him from calling her mom in front of others. She directed him to address her as Pastor. Eventually Les's wife did the cardinal sin: she complains about his behavior to mom and others. The immediate response from the inner circle was to blame her for the failed marriage to shut her up. His wife, like all of us, might not have been perfect, but she deserved to have a voice in the counseling sessions and to be heard.

Les's wife shouldered the blame for being forthcoming about her husband's affairs. Les often made comments referencing his wife's weight. According to his wife, he told her he was not going to have sex with something that looked like the back of an elephant. Les's wife was gradually ostracized from the church for speaking out while asking for help. She ultimately filed for divorce as she continued to voice her discontent about Les.

To counter and end the allegations against him, mom married Les to Serika within nine months of his divorce. It was unclear when mom tried to explain to me who Serika was. Les claimed to have met her while running an annual revival in Virginia. She won the hearts of the inner circle at the annual Fourth of July church picnic. Using what mom called Serika's spirit of discernment, Mom said, "Serika called out those spirits the way God showed them to her." She made inference to the choir vice president. Serika brought the choir vice president to the verge of tears by aggressively attacking his sexuality.

Mom went on to say Serika had one small child, and then some weeks later I was told, no, she had three children. From there I was told by mom she had a job with the Hilton Hotel chain and "she is up there." I was not sure what that meant, except mom said she would have to talk with her again to understand what she did with them. I was told by mom that in her testimonials Serika disclosed that her previous husband was taken out of their house at gunpoint and she had had a gun pointed at her head as well.

I asked mom what this was all about. Was this police? Mom replied with she did not know, that she would have to hear the story again. The church leadership regime said the marriage was from God and that was why it happened so quickly. Mom married them after a Sunday morning service during their annual holy convocation. Les's oldest daughter posted on Facebook when she heard the news of the wedding: "Another life ruined."

Before the ceremony, mom rebuked the church congregation for thinking negative about this marriage. She told them that they were going to accept Serika into the Tabernacle Church family, and if anyone didn't, they would have to deal with her. After mom said this, many in the congregation did not linger around for the wedding ceremony. Nine months passed before mom realized she had married Les to an ex-convict. Prior to marrying Les, Serika claimed she had a brain tumor and a year to live. She testified that the brain tumor melted away after mother prayed for her—only to find out Serika never had a brain tumor from the start. In or around May 2012, some former members from the Tabernacle Church discovered that Serika was in prison for five years prior to her marrying Minister Les. This came to light after Serika's aunt became angry about a personal matter between them. In order to validate the aunt's story about Serika's past, people initiated Google searches and inquiries as to who Serika was. The aunt said the brain tumor story was false. They surmised her twice-a-month trips to Virginia were to visit her probation officer.

After I informed mother about Serika's past, mom said in an e-mail to me, "About Serika, yes, I found out what type of person she is, but she will not be near my pocketbook or any personals of mine." Mother says to me, "I pray that God will help Lesley. My heart goes out to him, but prayer is the answer."

Sixteen months after the wedding, mother told Serika that she was releasing her from the Tabernacle Church and from Lesley. My understanding is Serika responded irritably, saying, "You can release me from your church, but you can't discharge me from my husband." Serika left the Tabernacle, vowing to never return, but not before she bamboozled Lesley's mother out of many thousands of dollars. Serika, somehow, secured power of attorney on Lesley's mother's personal business and credit card accounts.

The choir vice president also became a casualty to Serika by cosigning for her and Les to relocate to a luxurious apartment at Crystal Hills, Pomona, New York. The choir vice president told mom and the others that he was going to have Serika arrested and incarcerated for messing up his credit. The last time I saw Les, he looked to be tormented and estranged. The latest of memories about Serika and Lesley was shortly after their wedding. A preacher arrived at the Tabernacle pronouncing blessings while prophesying financial prosperity for both. The preacher proclaimed that God said Serika and Les would be multimillionaires. The parishioners hearing the prophecy began yelling hallelujahs and dancing down the sanctuary aisles uncontrollably.

Legalist pastors and church leadership regimes have taken a toll on many lives. If churches were to work with the balance and notion of becoming more spiritual, we could be better served. We could leave from church services, holding ourselves accountable to do better, with the help of God.

The helpless are not being helped in their very communities while the churches behave as if it's not their problem. Church leaderships are busy with their social agendas—Facebook postings, television reality shows, anniversaries, birthday revivals, show boating, etc. The leadership is tethered down to commitments that give the church a mispurpose, or no time to love thy neighbor. The church is underchurched. It appears that a great number of churches are ill fated, with all sense of reasoning gone from the four walls of the building.

Buyers, beware. Charismatic evangelical movements sometimes are started by angry ministers. And that anger passed downward to the people around them. Numerous ministers leave their home churches in conflict with the leadership with their focus on "I'll show them a thing or two." Have you ever been in awe of why some church folks are just hateful? Well, angry people pass forward their rage and spitefulness to folk who do not know how to rebuff it. When a minister is consistent with "God told me to do this and to do that," it gets scary. Does God really tell a minister every small detail that they say and do? For example, telling you where to place your furniture in your home. This style of church corporate leadership is what I consider to be authoritative and dictatorial. It can be dangerous in the hands of a lunatic. I think of Jim Jones, David Koresh, and others who made fatal decisions for people's lives. Absolute power and authority can be dangerous. Control and power can become very destructive to leaders and their flocks if it is not channeled correctly.

A spiritual person recognizes the tongue's power to build up or to tear down. The tongue only shapes the words that originate in our hearts and minds. Hearts that are of God's spirit and power produce speech that builds others up instead of tearing them down.

HOLINESS

WHAT IS *HOLINESS*? THIS IS the definition from Dictionay.com:

> Specially recognized as or declared sacred by religious use or authority; consecrated: holy ground. Dedicated or devoted to the service of God, the church, or religion. Having a spiritually pure quality, a holy love. In addition, Holiness is defined as one of the qualities of God and Jesus Christ. It should be a quality of Christians as well.

The Beatitudes

Matthew 5: When Jesus saw the crowds; he went up a mountain and sat down. His disciples came to him, and he began to teach them: Blessed are those who recognize they are spiritually helpless. The kingdom of heaven belongs to them.[4] Blessed are those who mourn. They will be comforted. Blessed are those who are gentle. They will inherit the earth. Blessed are those who hunger and thirst for God's approval. They will be satisfied. Blessed are those who show mercy. They will be treated mercifully. Blessed are those whose thoughts are pure. They will see God. Blessed are those who make peace. They will be called God's children. Blessed are those who are persecuted for doing what God approves of. The kingdom of heaven belongs to them. Blessed are you when people insult you, persecute you, lie, and say all kinds of evil things about you because of me. Rejoice and be glad because you have a great reward in heaven! The prophets who lived before you were persecuted in these ways.

God's People Make a Difference in the World

You are salt for the earth. But if salt loses its taste, how will it be made salty again? It is no longer good for anything except to be thrown out and trampled on by people. You are light for the world. A city cannot be hidden when it is located on a hill. No one lights a lamp and puts it under a basket. Instead, everyone who lights a lamp puts it on a lamp stand. Then its light shines on everyone in the house. In the same way let your light shine in front of people. Then they will see the good that you do and praise your Father in heaven.

Jesus Fulfills the Old Testament Scriptures

Don't ever think that I came to set aside Moses' Teachings or the Prophets. I didn't come to set them aside but to make them come true. I can guarantee this truth: Until the earth and the heavens disappear, neither a period nor a comma will disappear from the Scriptures before everything has come true. So whoever sets aside any command that seems unimportant and teaches others to do the same will be unimportant in the kingdom of heaven. But whoever does and teaches what the commands say will be called great in the kingdom of heaven. I can guarantee that unless you live a life that has God's approval and do it more faithfully than the experts in Moses' Teachings and Pharisees, you will never enter the kingdom of heaven.

Don't Do Good Works to Be Praised by People

Matthew 6: Be careful not to do your good works in public in order to attract attention. If you do, your Father in heaven will not reward you. So when you give to the poor, don't announce it with trumpet fanfare. This is what hypocrites do in the synagogues and on the streets in order to be praised by people. I can guarantee this truth: That will be their only reward. When you give to the poor, don't let your left hand know what your right hand is doing. Give your contributions privately. Your Father sees what you do in private. He will reward you.

The Lord's Prayer

When you pray, don't be like hypocrites. They like to stand in synagogues and on street corners to pray so that everyone can see them. I can guarantee this truth: That will be their only reward. When you pray, go to your room and close the door. Pray privately to your Father who is with you. Your Father sees what you do in private. He will reward you. When you pray, don't ramble like heathens who think they'll be heard if they talk a lot. Don't be like them. Your Father knows what you need before you ask him. This is how you should pray: Our Father in heaven, let your name be kept holy. Let your kingdom come. Let your will be done on earth as it is done in heaven. Give us our daily bread today. Forgive us as we forgive others. Don't allow us to be tempted. Instead, rescue us from the evil one. If you forgive the failures of others, your heavenly Father will also forgive you. But if you don't forgive others, your Father will not forgive your failures.

Stop Judging

Matthew 7: Stop judging so that you will not be judged. Otherwise, you will be judged by the same standard you use to judge others. The standards you use for others will be applied to you. So why do you see the piece of sawdust in another believer's eye and not notice the wooden beam in your own eye? How can you say to another believer, 'Let me take the piece of sawdust out of your eye,' when you have a beam in your own eye? You hypocrite! First remove the beam from your own eye. Then you will see clearly to remove the piece of sawdust from another believer's eye.

The Golden Rule

Always do for other people everything you want them to do for you. That is the meaning of Moses' Teachings and the Prophets.

False Prophets

Beware of false prophets. They come to you disguised as sheep, but in their hearts they are vicious wolves. You will know them by what they produce. "People don't pick grapes from thorn bushes or figs from thistles, do they? In the same way every good tree produces good fruit, but a rotten tree produces bad fruit. A good tree cannot produce bad fruit, and a rotten tree cannot produce good fruit. Any tree that fails to produce good fruit is cut down and thrown into a fire. So you will know them by what they produce. Not everyone who says to me, 'Lord, Lord!' will enter the kingdom of heaven, but only the person who does what my Father in heaven wants. Many will say to me on that day, 'Lord, Lord, didn't we prophesy in your name? Didn't we force out demons and do many miracles by the power and authority of your name?' Then I will tell them publicly, 'I've never known you. Get away from me, you evil people.'"

As I end this chapter, I can't help but think that there are churches spinning and spewing undeodorized dogma through microphones and over pulpits Sunday after Sunday. If you think of these teachings in stark contrast, as their polar opposite, their meaning allows us to understand unwanted pain and suffering. It is as if ministers are feeding God's sheep red meat, making them more contemptible with each sermon. A mean-spirited sermon delivered to believing people will manifest itself through their behavior and actions. We can't earn our way to God; we can't self-sacrifice our way to God. We have to trust in the work that Jesus did on the cross. God's rewards are in heaven. We can also have a better life on this earth based on how we live here. God rewards holiness. Without holiness, no one will see God. Holiness is so paramount that God sent his Son to die on a cross so that we can work toward it, and attain it.

One of my readers sent this article to me that I found to be interesting. The article was written in November 2013 by William J. Alston, unrelated to me as far as I know:

> Recently I saw an interview on BET with a rap superstar and a high profile, well liked and admired megachurch pastor. The pastor asked the rapper was he a Christian in which the rapper responded "Yes, cause I pay my tithes!" causing the pastor to nod his head and remark…"With you that must be some TITHE!." There was not one mention of you must be born-again, of denying yourself taking up your cross and following Christ, of repentance and believing the gospel…ABSOLUTELY NOTHING! I cut off the TV grieved knowing that possible millions were watching that interview with many given the impression that a person can buy their way into heaven, live any way you like but give God that coin and you're okay. Deception is rampant in these days. Make no mistake—THE WAGES OF SIN IS DEATH BUT THE GIFT OF GOD IS ETERNAL LIFE THROUGH JESUS CHRIST OUR Lord. (Romans 6:23)

Holiness is far less complicated than understanding the religious rituals we subject ourselves to as we move toward Judgment Day.

CALLED TO BE A PK
(PASTOR'S KID)

CHURCH IN MY FAMILY WAS front and center! According to the late leadership expert Peter Drucker, pastoring ranks as one of the four hardest jobs in America. Ranking in no specific order would be the president of the United States, CEO of a hospital, university president, and a pastor. I believe it does not have to be one of the hardest jobs just because we say it is. It appears that pastors take on a highlighted pleasure about touting they are a pastor. In other words, "See! I told ya'll my job is hard! This is why I am stressed out and overworked. Now you may pity me. When is my appreciation service?" No witticism intended.

Pastoring shouldn't be as hard as pastors make it. In this modern day, if a pastor feels they are under the same pressure as the Apostle Paul, a lot of it has to be self-inflicted hardship. In most cases this hardship that a pastor may feel is passed onto their spouses, children, friends, and others to endure.

The Associated Press reported a story on June 9, 2012: "The 15-year-old daughter of mega church Pastor Creflo Dollar told authorities her father choked and punched her, and hit her with his shoe during an argument over whether she could go to a party, according to a police report." Family values are irreplaceable. If I had but one prayer while growing into adulthood, it would have been the following:

Have family discussions. Avoid using sarcasm.

Talk openly with each other.

Work together to solve difficult family problems. Be kind to each other.

Get "I love you" hugs.

Get encouragement that you can be or do anything you want.

Share our spiritual values and beliefs with each other.

Growing up, it would have thrilled me to see dad hug mom, and mom hugging dad. Possibly mom and dad sitting close to each other or driving down the road as I saw other couples in the sixties and seventies sitting on the car seat almost looking like one person. I don't recall seeing that as a youngster or an adult. What I see now are staged poses of framed photographs on the end tables in the family room.

Being a family is important. If I could have impeded people from being intrusive, exploiting our privacy and taking up tenancy in our home, I would have. We lived in a small one-bedroom house, one bathroom with an attic transformed into two small low-ceiling rooms for me, my sister, and younger brother. We usually had some person that my mother had taken in living with us almost all the time. I can bring to mind one person in particular, a woman who was mentally ill with all the tendencies of her condition. She walked around throughout the night talking incoherently, answering to voices she thought she was hearing, speaking in tongues, demanding demons to leave the house while shaking her fist in the air. It was only God that kept us safe. The lady had free access to roam the house, including the kitchen where the knives or a variety of other select tools to harm us while we slept were kept.

My mother's zeal to have a church and to save folk from their sin took precedent over her immediate family's safety. I and my siblings wandered through abandonment and social seclusion because of mom—with some real disconnect to social norms and mores of a family. Childhood is too precious and valuable a time not to have proper nurturing and guidance. In my household, rules were very strict for me and my siblings. Mom laid out the law and we followed it. Being the only child for nine years, mother insisted my friends had to be saved and Christian. Church attendance was more important to mom than it was for me. We went to church five to six days a week, sometimes seven, including school nights when church would go on until midnight. If it came down to church, sports, or other school activities, church won out hands down.

I used to dread Sundays. It was an all-day church affair, from sunup until sundown. Churches we attended never seem to start on time or end at a decent hour. Mom told me after many years of being a pastor, "I need to keep people on their knees and in the church. This keeps them out of trouble." I was not permitted to go to my prom, dances, movies, parties, and certain school activities. Only select gospel music was allowed to be listened to. I was not allowed to go to the movies because mother said I would be sitting in the seat of scorners. Out of frustration I once said, "How about when you ride on a bus or eat in a restaurant." That was one of my fatal mistakes. I got the whipping of my life.

I was born out of wedlock and found this out through my own research after I became an adult. Initially, mom denied the fact until I showed her my birth certificate alongside the marriage certificate. My parents were very young when I was born. My mother had just turned fifteen. I was told by relatives she tried different ways to abort the pregnancy. Her defense to this, not that she needed one, was, "At least, all of you had the same father."

I believe through the divine plan of birth my being here has a purpose, as for all our lives there is a purpose. For the most part, I cannot say I was neglected or abused during my childhood. At best I was kept on the straight and narrow with switches and belts to my backside by my mother. "A rod and a reprimand impart wisdom, but a child left undisciplined disgraces its mother" (Proverb 29:15 NIV).

My mother was a product of child abuse, along with not knowing anything about her biological father. I can see the profound effect this has had on her. Even though she says it's all right, I know it's not.

Many Pentecostal worshippers say when their family life is not good, "Jesus is my father, mother, brother, and sister." Sometime they would say he is a "doctor in the operating room or a lawyer in the courtroom.

Jesus is all I need." There are some single women that say Jesus is their husband. I have yet to hear a single man say Jesus is his wife.

There are thousands of women and men sitting in church pews, standing in pulpits every Sunday. Men and women masking their hurt and trauma brought on by some type of abuse that was no fault of their own. Suppressing hurt, shame, and embarrassment by not knowing how to obtain therapy can be passed forward onto future generations. Giving children a nurturing environment and foundation to mature in is vital. Leaving pain and hurt unfixed until Jesus comes can lead people into extreme legalistic religious worship.

I vividly remember the day my mother said she found Jesus. She came home and threw away her albums, even her favorite artist Jackie Wilson, who she loved and adored. She threw away my dad's rock 'n' roll 45s. All alcoholic beverages went down the kitchen drain.

As a child I was left in a conundrum and baffled when my mother abruptly altered her lifestyle, doing a complete one-eighty. My dad was no longer allowed to smoke in the house, and in those days it wasn't the secondhand smoke. Mother preached to my father continually that smoking is a sin unto God. Dad continued smoking in the yard, then in the detached garage. When mother turned up the burners on dad's smoking in the yard, Dad started smoking secretly away from home. With mother in hot pursuit of his habit, he finally gave it up all together and gave his heart to God. But not before she kept him awake many nights speaking in tongues. In time I understood that this abrupt turn about was brought on by mom professing repentance. Mom said she was saved by the blood of Jesus Christ, sanctified, and filled with the Holy Ghost with fire. My mother said she was a new creature in God, born again from her sins and iniquity.

A few years later, mom said she was called into the ministry by God to feed his sheep. My mother has always proclaimed that if God did not call her she would not be doing what she is doing. Many times she has told her congregation, "If you did not give me anything, I would still honor my call from God." She has often said that if she did not have food, God would send the raven to feed her.

Our home was usually filled with mayhem—church and more church, strange people coming into our home saying they were part of our family. Preachers and singing groups would come and go. I gave up my bed to men and women who said they were sent by God—at least that was what I was told. I have down pat a preacher by the name of Elder Jamison and his quiet skillful piano-playing wife. They stayed with us for about a month or longer. I was not sure where these two people came from or where they were going. Mom would take Elder Jamison into relatives' and friends' homes where he would preach to them. When Elder Jamison preached, it would be an emotional time. I would see people welt up as tears flowed down their cheeks. The expressions he used convicted them of the sin and guilt they carried.

After Elder Jamison preached, he'd make an altar call. I remember going to a rooming house with my mother, Elder Jamison, his wife, and others. It was a large open room with about nine or so beds, all occupied by men. This large dorm room was located on a second floor, on North Main Street, Spring Valley, New York. There had to be about fifteen men attending this service. After they accepted Christ in their hearts, Elder Jamison would customarily yell out, "Fill the tub." Then he would say, "You must go down and be baptized in water, in Jesus's name." At the end he would eloquently ask for donations, where they all gave liberally.

Long after they left, my mother found out that Elder Jamison came from Florida. The talented piano-playing woman he was with was not his legitimate wife but a woman he ran away with from his home church in Florida. Mom tried to explain to me that Elder Jamison was a "Jesus Only" Pentecostal. Mom said there was no biblical standing for "Jesus Only" Pentecostal folks.

Let me not forget the kissing evangelist by the name of Inez. No hand laying on people's foreheads. Inez's thing was kissing or blowing on people and they would fall onto the ground. I remember she told the congregation. "I have never met or seen a man yet that was saved below their belt buckle." After she said that, I figured out why she never kissed men.

And then there was the evangelist who said he had anointed oil running from the palm of his hands as he held them up to the congregation. I could not get past the picture of looking at a man perspiring profusely from head to toe. The preacher came down from the pulpit, standing in front of the altar with his white shirt drenched with sweat, with the tail of the shirt hanging loosely from his trousers. He stood holding the palm of his hands up to the congregation as he convinced them he had anointed holy oil coming from his palms. He told the congregation it was a gift from God. He suggested they come up, form a line, and allow him to lay his hands on their heads. He said they would be blessed from the oil running from the palm of his hands.

Then there was Elder Matthew and his wife from Jamaica, who spoke with a heavy accent. Elder Matthew appeared to be in constant need of something that anybody or somebody could do for him. I noticed they were not large offering givers but stood willingly to accept more than they put in the offering pail. It sometimes seemed like they did not know when to go back home, wearing their welcome out in our house.

And Gerry, Gerry was a delightful guy. He came to the church when he was young. I was the first church organist for the Tabernacle Church, followed by Gerry who was a much better organist than me. He was naturally gifted without ever reading music. I left home for college and do remember the church taking up an offering for me on my last Sunday service. It was about $350, and being the early 1970s, I was extremely thankful. Gerry was intuitive to mom's unnatural and excessive need for attention early on in their relationship. He was the church clown—pudgy, round faced, and mannered. He preferred spending his time with the ladies and girls rather than being with the menfolk. His popularity was when he would turn into this comic character, making fun of other people. Gerry and mom would laugh at people and the style of worship of some of the congregants.

He lived with our family for two or three years in our basement. He would tell everyone he was mom's son, calling her mom. He entertained mom at the kitchen table after church services. He would mock how people talked, how they walked, what they looked like. Gerry would stand up from the chair he was sitting on and start mocking and imitating folks doing their holy dance, or rolling around on the floor. Gerry ran the full gambit when it came to mocking worshipers. Sitting on the Hammond organ bench he had a full focal view of everything that went on. After he lived with us, mom and the inner circle allowed him to live at the church. Everything was going well until someone decided to rat him out. They found pornographic magazines of men in sexual positions in his living quarters at the church and reported it to mom. Mom went down to the church, grabbed a mop handle, and started beating Gerry. He left Tabernacle Church after this, moving to Newark, New Jersey. To make a living, he contracted himself out to play for various churches. Sadly, some years later Gerry passed away with the HIV virus. After Gerry was driven from the living quarters of the church, a lady called Mother Cuna moved in with her husband. Mother Cuna and her husband were from Jamaica. She was a slender woman, about six feet tall, wearing black frame glasses. When she smiled, you could not help but notice her sparkling gold tooth. That one tooth when struck by incandescent lighting was like a flash of lightning in her mouth. Mother Cuna had a wonderful disposition, unlike her husband. Mr. Cuna was less tall, standing at the height of Mother Cuna's shoulders. He never spoke, just a quick nod of his head with a faint low mumble that sounded like "huh." I was never sure what he really said. Mom said it was good to have someone at the church to watch out for the building. Folks living at the church lived rent free for years.

Mom would get infuriated and downright mad when Mr. Cuna would cook Jamaican food on some Sundays and the aroma would resonate through the entire church during the Sunday worship services. From what I could see, Mr. Cuna ignored mom and the inner circle, and pretty well cooked when he wanted to. Mr. Cuna never attended church while they occupied the illegal apartment over the sanctuary. I remember Mother Cuna making a delicious carrot juice for mom after she preached. Mother Cuna would send gallons of carrot juice home with mom's nurses and adjutants. Eventually Mother Cuna and her husband retired. They relocated to Florida where they built from the ground up a beautiful luxurious ranch-style home for themselves.

Among other people we had to tolerate in the house was a youth minister by the name of Waddell from Baltimore, Maryland. In his midtwenties, he visited often, making claim he was part of our family. Waddell always stayed with us while he ran a youth revival at the Tabernacle. One time his visit was abruptly interrupted by my dad. Giving him five minutes to collect his belonging and vacate the premises, my dad inharmoniously demanded him to leave one morning. I never learned my father's reason. I did learn he had impregnated one of the church's underage girls on one of his revival running visits. Youth minister Waddell died in later years with the HIV virus. These are just a few of the people I met in my youth.

PASTOR'S KIDS SPEAK OUT

CHECK OUT THIS INTERNET POSTING from www.churchleaders. com in January 2014, "What It's Really Like to Be a PK."

Seven major things pastors wanted you to know about their children. The article had a big response when it was first posted. But, for reasons I have not completely fathomed, the post went viral a few weeks ago. Now almost 200,000 views and hundreds of comments later, we can see a pretty clear picture. You see, the majority of those who responded were pastors' kids. So, instead of hearing from pastors about their children, we heard directly from the children themselves. Some were teenagers still living with their parents. Others were adults who grew up as PKs. All of them had pretty strong opinions. As I read again through the plethora of comments, I developed seven major themes from these PKs. Not all of their comments were negative, but a majority did communicate some level of pain.

Here is what they said:

1. *The glass house is a reality.* **People are always looking at the PKs. They have trouble saying or doing anything without someone, usually a church member, making a comment. Most of these PKs (and former PKs) felt a great deal of discomfort living in the glass house. Some even expressed bitterness.**

2. *Some church members made a positive and lasting impression on PKs.* **One of the more frequent positive comments we heard was about the church members who loved and cared for the PKs. Many of them took the children under their wings and made a positive difference in their lives.**

   My dad has been a pastor for 26 yrs and I've grown up in that glass house. Though he always has put our family first and said that we should not be held to any higher standard than any other Christian. He would say he was called into the ministry not us. I've dealt with both the good and the bad members, seen my parents, myself, and my siblings attacked. I've tried not to let the bad apples spoil my Christian walk. <u>Clinton Garsee</u>

   Greetings to all PK's, my heart goes out to each of you for all that you have given up and suffered through the years that you walked with your parents in the obedience to the Lord. There is no question that you have faced sometimes more pressure than your parents did in their respective ministries. If there is one thing the enemy hates more the pastors then that is pastors' kids, no matter what age they are. I appreciate your honesty and your openness to be real on this forum; it has given me great insight into how to be a parent and a pastor. I hope and pray that each of you who are PK's will always remember that the Lord loves you dearly and has a great plan for each of you individually. I pray that if you have any hurt from things that you saw, heard and experienced first hand, you would be able to forgive and use those things to make you stronger men and women of God. You are truly the love of your parents' life and if they made mistakes when you were young they would change them if they could and do things differently for sure.

I am a missionary Pastor with 6 sons, I made many mistakes as a young Pastor that I would change if I could but that I will not make with my younger kids. The Lord has blessed me to have made it through some hard times with my older sons and now I see the Lord working in their lives in a great way. I bless each of you in the name of the Lord.

Thank you for your insight. During our 3 children's childhood I served as a church planting missionary in Europe, pastoral ministry in Canada, and teaching at a Bible College back in Europe. Our daughter (37) is an associate member with a mission agency and leads every two years a team on European mission trips. 2nd son is active in another church. Youngest son and family attends our church. But the reality that PKs leave the church is real. Mostly, it is the church who does not accept them just normal regular kids. 3 out of 4 of our lead pastor's kids are not walking with Jesus. <u>Christoph Koebel</u>

I was a p/k. Yes we lived in a glass house. Anything that happened someone was always watching I and my siblings. I could not attend my honors banquet my junior year of high school because it interfered with Wednesday night church. I did talk my dad into letting me attend my senior year however. If the church doors were open we were expected to be there. And there was no kids club/ you sat in church with the adults Sunday morning and Sunday night and Wed night. However I learned a lot of respect by sitting there and I learned how to be quiet. I have a problem with some now days that let their children run around the church or talk during the church service. We had to sit with my mother until we were teenagers or at least close and if you made a sound we heard it after service.

I loved the old hymns and still do. The modern music is fine but I think we are losing some of the older hymns that are so beautiful to sing. As a p/k I always had to wear dresses to church and school. My father said I had to set a good example for the others. Not sure what wearing a dress had to do with it. But that was the rule.

We were supposed to set aside Saturday night as family night. We were all expected to be home but quite a bit of the time my father was making a call or got called out.

Maybe it was the pressure of being a minister that finally took a toll on my parents' marriage and they divorced when I was in my early 20s due to an affair my father had with the church organist who he later married. I have a hard time trusting ministers because I have seen so many that all they want is money, wealth and fame. And some lead double lives, as did my father for a few years. Silvia A.

Sadly, I too identify with most of these comments and some that haven't been mentioned. I have always felt that during my parents tenured as pastors I neither had parents nor pastors. I must say that as an adult my parents are trying to repair this effect on me growing up but it does feel awkward. I thank God that He had mercy on me to repair the hurt that was inflicted on me and that He has had grace with me to still use me a vessel to minister to others. Thank you for validating what was inflicted on "kids" that should have been loved by the church family.

I was a pk and I'm still in music ministry though not church related. At 49 yrs. old I find it difficult to trust church people. I church hop never wanting to really trust anyone. My folks had few close friends at their churches mostly because the people that acted like their best buds were the ones reporting all they heard and said to the higher ups in the denomination. I dislike the church in general but love my savior Jesus Christ.

As a pastor I appreciate this so much. As a pastor of two teens, it's easy to get caught up in the ministry to others and forget that our first ministry is to our family. I have always attempted to put my children first over ministry. Not my personal relationship with Jesus, but ministry things that come up. I've not always been successful, but my children know how much they mean to me. I've been criticized by church members for this, but in the end it doesn't really matter to me what a cranky member thinks about my family choices. They will be my children a lot longer than someone will be my church member. Be blessed I was 17 when a rumor was flying around the local high school (that I didn't even attend) that my dad was forcing I and my girlfriend to get married because I had knocked her up. A few weeks later, a lady in our congregation thought she saw us kissing and flipped her lid. People in church can definitely be total jerks. That being said, I am now in full-time ministry. As a pastor's kid, I think I'm better suited for ministry because I have thick skin. I've learned that people can be awful, but I'm not here for them. I'm here for the rich soil, for the good ground. When people are ridiculous, I just laugh about it. It doesn't surprise me anymore.

This just makes me sad. Yes I have been one of those who judged too harshly and held PK's to a higher standard, but as I have grown in grace I have also learned to give grace. Over the past decade I have tried hard to make a real effort to support, encourage, love and give grace to not only the PK but also the PW (Pastor's Wife). They need our prayers, our grace, our love and support.

I think the hardest thing for me as a PK was when work was brought home. It was hard knowing or overhearing confidential information but not being able to talk with anyone about it. Even as a teenager I had to be careful who I talked to about my very normal adolescent frustrations with my parents because I feared painting them in the wrong light. The thing I'm still bitter about is seeing my parents deserted or betrayed by someone they had opened their life to and who we thought were our lifelike friends. I have lost many very close and best friends because their parents left our church.

On a positive note, my parents did a phenomenal job raising me to stick with God no matter what. Unlike a lot of pastors' kids, I never had a "rebellious period" and I definitely wasn't a devil child. I loved being involved on ministry with my parents and it instilled in me that family should be ministering together as a unified unit.

In retrospect, I love that I was a PK. It had its ups and downs, but it prepared me for ministry as an adult. Not to mention that my parents were great parents and great pastors!

Good job on the article—most seems pretty accurate! But everyone and every situation is different!

I'm a pk and my experience has been parents at a distance. My relationship with my father suffered a lot because of the balance between ministry and us. Plus I grew up in a time when legalistic service was common. I even ran from God's calling on my life just because of this. I wanted no part of something that would take all of you like that. I acted out with anger and hate. I lived up to the stereotypical pk as much as possible. So for the Lord to pull me out of my mess and misunderstandings about the calling and who God is was very humbling and world shattering. I feel for pks in a very special way—be blessed and a blessing. <u>Drae</u>

Thank you for this article. As a young pastor with young children, we have a lot ahead of us as a family. I am terrified that my kids will grow up bitter towards the church. Our church family is amazing and they all love my kids, but it can only take one or two comments to really create a wound. I am just have to try to be intentional about raising them and putting my family before the church.

As a grown pk who did not grow up resenting the church, my advice to you is to involve your children instead of ignoring them, give them choices, explain things as best you can to them as they see things they may not understand, and the one thing, I'll never forget that my father taught me—god first, family second, church third. God does not equal ministry— he is in ministry, but the ministry or church itself is not God. Remember to differentiate the two. <u>Rev. Dr. Harvey Carr</u>

I was a PK and hated that the only times I ever saw my dad were when he was in the pulpit and when he came home to discipline me if I had done something wrong, or something he had heard I might have done wrong. My mom had a standing joke on Sundays, "Wave at your dad so he will know who you are." My dad was from the generation who were taught in school your ministry belonged to the church 24/7 and your family had to accept it. Sadly they still taught that when I was in college and seminary, but soon learned the fallacy of that teaching. The judgment of PK's was unrelenting. I remember a teen boy, a year younger than me being disciplined at school for getting caught shooting craps on the schoolyard. His mother came to my home and told my mom her son had never known anything about dice until he started playing board games with me! (To this day I know nothing about gambling with dice or cards.) Yet, her son had a reputation for the use of alcohol (in a dry state), improper relations with the girls, a real bully, etc. He certainly learned none of those things in my home. And, I could not have taught him elsewhere as my parents did not allow me to go anywhere but church and school. Our friends had to come to our house to play board games. (We were not allowed to have cards.) I did not even have my first date until a freshman in college away from home! SB

I am a PK who married a PK. We have both experienced horrific encounters with church people. I had a church member verbally assault me in front of the church while my parents weren't around. For the first time, I decided to speak out for myself. It came back on my parents. Even though nothing I said was wrong and everyone there said my comment was nothing but honest and appropriate. The person who was saying things about me tried to take the fact that I would say anything as a slight against my parents and their ability to minister. That caused me to shut down and shut church people out. I went through a phase in college where I wouldn't go to church and it felt like I could finally breathe not looking over my shoulder at church. I am in and in a position of leadership. I watch out for all PKs and leaders kids because people like to think they are fair game. Dr. T

I'm sorry but I see a different picture. Kids period should be taught to be respectful. PK kids have demonstrated some of the worst behaviors just like other kids. But Pastors' children think that they can push the envelope and get away with more because they are the pastors kids. I have watched first hand pk kids acting horribly and no one says anything because they are put on a mini pedestal like the pastor himself. Pk kids are special but they too play a role in their horrible behavior.

I'm sorry, but this is a blatant stereotyping of PK's. As a Pastor, I have always approached it this way, Pastors' KIDS are still KIDS. Mine are respectful, responsible and have rarely, if ever caused attention to be drawn to themselves by their behavior. My kids know that I have a standard they are to live up to, as their DAD, not their Pastor. We actually had this very discussion with our daughter last year. She felt as though she couldn't do something or wear something just because she was a Pastor's daughter. I simply took away the Pastor from the conversation and she realized her dad has certain standards of behavior or dress that would exist even if he was a Walmart greeter. While I have seen what you are describing, it isn't only limited to PK's nor does it exist in ALL PK's. I think you over generalized and that is what I'm attempting to address. Be blessed.

I understand your point of view. I was a horrible teenager (even for a PK) but a great deal of my rebellion and behavior was rooted in my insecurities as an adolescent (no different from any other kid of my age) and some serious psychological damage that was caused by my experience in the church. This damage wasn't addressed until just a few years ago (in my early 30s.) Imagine being a teenager who has to grow up with everyone watching you. Expectations about who you should be, where you should go, what you should wear, what career you should pursue, are rampant. Every time you mess up, even a little, there is a line of people waiting to tell you, "Really, you're the pastor's kid, you should know better." Now, add to that the difficulties inherent in being part of your parents' ministry. You learn things about other people in the church that you're not really old enough to understand fully, but you know are bad. People take their anger with your parents out on you because you're a safer target. Even though your pastor-parent may be going through an incredibly difficult situation (burnout, satanic oppression, depression, etc.) you can't talk to anyone about it for fear that they would think badly about your parent or your family. You feel like you can't trust ANYONE. I defy you to find a child who can handle that and not act horribly at least occasionally.

Until you've lived as a PK and endured the pressure to be "perfect" in the eyes of the congregation, you shouldn't give such a strong opinion. I love my parents and I have some good memories of the church we were in while I was growing up, but my parents were under such great pressure from the congregation that it bled off onto my sisters and I. Shame on you for downgrading that pressure to be perfect that people like yourself place on PKs like me.

Hearing someone's deep pain, and justifying more beatings, is an interesting approach.

I'm grateful that my parents were very protective of us and kept us from the scoundrels. I will never forget an instance where someone was attempting to correct us by saying "you know better than that you are pastors children." My mother who was in another conversation at the time, placed her conversation on hold to address the man speaking to us and said, "they are children and their parents happen to be pastors, don't isolate them like that." Although there were others who tried, we always felt important to them. It was always God, family, church and we knew it. Their prioritizing us made it easier when they had to go away.

3. **Some church members were jerks to the PKs**. Many of the stories are heartbreaking. It is really hard to imagine some of the awful words that were said to the PKs. Some still feel the sting of those words decades later.

4. **Many PKs resent the interrupted meals and vacations**. They felt like their pastor parent put the church before the family. One PK, now an adult, lamented that every vacation his family took was interrupted; and many times the vacation was truncated.

5. **Some of the PKs have very positive memories of when their parents included them in the ministry.** I read comments about hospital visits, nursing home visits and ministry in the community. These PKs absolutely loved doing ministry with mom and dad. They felt like the church ministry was something the whole family did.

6. **A key cry from the PKs was: "Let me be a regular kid."** A number of the PKs expressed pain from the high expectations placed upon them by both their parents and church members. Others said that some church members expected them to behave badly because that's just what PKs do.

7. **Some PKs left the church for good because of their negative experiences.** They viewed local congregations as a place for judgmental Christians who are the worst of hypocrites. They have no desire ever to return. You can feel the resentment and pain in their comments. Their hurt is palpable.

On the one hand, I feel badly for the opening of wounds that blog post caused. On the other hand, I am grateful for the forum it allowed for many of the PKs to express themselves.

If you are a PK, do you identify with these comments? How do the rest of you react to their hopes and hurts?

WADE IN THE WATERS

AFTER FINALLY SUCCUMBING TO THE dreaded disease of colon cancer, in 1983 my dad passed away. Ironically or coincidentally, he died on the exact day of mom's pastoral anniversary celebration at a little after two in the afternoon. A few years after my father's untimely death, my mother asked me if I could find the time to help her with the church. My answer was, "Of course." Unbeknownst to me, this answer came with an onset of unexpected troubled waters and experiences. While I still remain a member of the church, my attendance fell off. After Father died, I started the Alston-Scott educational scholarship foundation in honor of him, Deacon James Alston Sr. and Deacon John M. Scott, who was a loyalist to my mother's ministry. Under my guidance, the scholarship program was helpful to a number of students. Once my attendance at Tabernacle fell off, the church leadership regime took the scholarship program to Death Valley where it was never resurrected again.

The Tabernacle Church was established and incorporated for over thirty-five years prior to my rejoining the organization. I was returning somewhat older, wiser, balding, and definitely grayer with the passing years.

The first order of business was when I met with mom at her dining room table. She said she wanted to expand and remodel the church. With my business background I did not see this as a big problem to lend my expertise. First, it was my mom, and second, it was a church that I had grown up in. By my own right I love the church and the folks that worshipped there.

As Mom laid out the scope of work she envisioned, I took detailed notes and made drawings while we sat at the table. Once I had the vision of what she wanted done, I went to work by calling for a 9:00 p.m. midweek trustee meeting. The meeting took place a week later at mom's dining room table. Prior to the meeting I had requested the trustees bring all bank statements and accounts payables, what they had for cash on hand, and a few other items for review going back two years.

My rationale was simply that churches start large construction projects only to run short on funds to complete them or to have them stall. Far too often I have seen churches with oxidized steel sticking up from the ground for years. I needed to be sure this was not going to be the case for Tabernacle Church.

In attendance was mom, Reverend Helen, her husband who was the head of the trustee board, and Tessy who was a board member. The head trustee was a tall, dark, handsome man. I was taken aback when I last saw him. His face and neck was patterned with sores and some type of cysts. I asked him what was going on. He replied, "I have a blood disorder, and the doctor removes the cysts by using laser treatment." After his response, I moved on.

I had already calculated an estimated cost for the project based on the scope of work mom wanted done. The biggest and most costly parts of the project was extending the sanctuary by fifty feet and constructing a choir loft in the rear of the new addition behind the pulpit. I asked Reverend Helen and her husband how much money we had to work with. Reverend Helen stuttered in a very low voice, "A-about a hundred." I could barely hear her as she spoke.

I repeated what I thought she said, "About a hundred?" She nervously said, "Yes." I continued with the presentation, giving account of the approximate cost and scope of the work. I noticed Reverend Helen twitching, looking somewhat apprehensive with loud, reverberating sounds coming from her stomach. I asked her if she was hungry. She answered softly, "No, no." I then forged ahead with the details of the project. As I was summing up, I turned to Reverend Helen and said, "About one hundred thousand is what we have on hand?" She responded by saying softly, "About one hundred dollars." Surprised, I repeated, "One hundred dollars?"

At this point I looked around the table at the three of them, and then to my left where my mother sat at the head of the table. I said, "Did you say about one hundred dollars?" Tessy said nothing, just giving me a blank stare through her black rimmed glasses.

After years of being in the business of saving souls and passing the offering plate around, they confirmed the church treasury was about one hundred dollars. The most shocking was the board's acceptance of this as normal business practice. I looked at mom a second time. She looked distressed to find out after thirty-some years of her preaching and teaching, there was only about one hundred dollars on hand. My initial thought was there has to be some kind of oversight. I asked for all the invoices and bank statements. I started to filter through the church bills, lease agreements for equipment, etc. I tallied the offerings for each month. I wrote down what money came in and what money went out. Reverend Helen looked at me while I was busy with my calculator and said, "You do this a lot?" My busy response was, "Yeah, I do."

When we adjourned the meeting, it was after 4:00 a.m. My preliminary finding showed thousands of dollars unaccounted for. One year the numbers reflected the church paying out more than was collected in the offering plate.

I found ambiguous contracts with unfair lease agreements, disorganized paperwork, all compounded by a messy filing system. For example, the church was leasing two Pitney Bowes stamp machines for years that were not being used. They were behind on every monthly bill—electric and gas, radio broadcast, mortgage, everything! Using cash from the Sunday's church offerings, Reverend Helen and her husband were going to Orange and Rockland Utilities some Mondays to pay the bill just to keep the lights on.

A week later, I called a second meeting with the same group. After digging even further into the finances of the church, I followed the audit path to wherever it took me. The pattern was quite clear. The church was missing large sums of money. I told them there is a gross violation of church trust and antitrust violations within the organization. After I laid out my finding to my mother and the three board members, the head trustee handed me a bunch of hanging file folders with invoices, right side up, upside down, going in an assortment of directions. He said he had kept them in his attic over the years. I politely gave them back to him saying these items should be stored at the church, not at your house. The head trustee said to me, "I don't want ya'll to think that we are taking anything." I never acknowledged his statement. At the end of the meeting, mom asked me to join the trustee board as a member. I accepted the offer. I went to work immediately to stop the bleeding, to protect the church and my mother from the losses and the situations that had been created.

A few months later the head trustee passed away from blood disease. Upon his passing, mom asked me to assume the role of head trustee, which I did, changing the position to chief administrator of Church Corporate Affairs. The church's corporate operation was in such disarray I asked my sister if she could lend a hand as well.

She agreed, dropping things from her already busy schedule to help out. Since she was finishing up her degree, she made it clear her schoolwork had to continue. I understood. I was just happy to have her legal and business expertise. I would have called on my younger brother, but he lived in Virginia and was finishing his master's degree. I instituted weekly trustee meet-ings every Tuesday after prayer service. I made sure the agenda contained time for members with advance notice to present ideas or pressing issues to the trustee board. All board meeting minutes were given to Mother at the close of each meeting.

It took approximately six months for my sister and me, along with Tessy and three other board members to clean up the backlog of unpaid bills. The trustee office had one huge metal desk with stacks of papers, loose ledger journals, and invoices covering the desktop. Behind the desk was a padded wooden chair with a slatted back. The desk was encircled by four metal folding chairs for other trustees. Directly across the room from this metal desk sits a large combination floor safe. My sister immediately ordered several new desks and chairs for every board member. We also moved the trustee board office into another room that was more work friendly.

Six months in, we had five thousand dollars saved and all outstanding invoices were paid. The parishioners were supportive, and within one year's time we had $150,000 to move forward with the new renovations. The next two steps were to find an architect to draw the design and a contractor that could build the architect's plans. I went to work interviewing architects and contractors. The trustee board agreed on an architect with high ratings from Piermont, New York.

The contractors were a little more difficult to line up. The structure required wood and steel framing, with cement columns supporting the flooring. The addition extended over the parking lot by fifty feet to a height of eighteen feet. The architect's drawing called for nine cement columns with footings four feet underground. My initial reaction to the architect was the amount of steel for the addition appeared to be overdesigned and overengineered. After several meetings and discussions with me, the trustee board, contractor, and building inspector, we came to the conclusion that it was overengineered; however, we were attaching the new addition to a building that was built in the early 1870s. The general idea was to make the addition an independent self-sustaining structure as the older structure could not bear the weight of the addition. When the two exteriors and interiors were joined with smooth transition lines, they would be independent of each other with the addition able to withstand any natural disaster or storm.

Before we could start construction, there were two more hurdles. The first involved getting unanimous approval for the project from the village planning board. Taking a great deal of time and many village town hall meetings, it was one of the toughest planning boards I had dealt with. Now keep in mind Mother had been in the village for well over thirty years. I remember the last meeting before we received approval. Speaking to the minds, hearts, and soul of the planning board, I recall saying, "If you don't allow us to do this, you basically are telling the pastor, who is my mother, to pack up and get out of town because we don't want you here." I asked the board membership, "How many people maybe didn't get robbed or your home broken into because of the church being here? How many people are not on drugs because of the church being here?" I went on with a litany of intangibles that could have happened if it wasn't for the church. Planning board members listened attentively, and one started weeping uncontrollably while saying, "It's not me that is voting no. Why are you all looking at me?"

A few weeks after this meeting, the approval from the planning board arrived. At this point only one hurdle remained. I contacted a bank representative and invited them to a trustee board meeting because we needed to borrow $150,000 to cover the cost of the construction, which was exceeding $300,000. This was barring any unforeseen problems. I know from experience that once you open up walls on older structures, you are going to run into unanticipated problems. What those problems are, you just don't know until you get into the actual demolition and construction. Sure enough we had many problems and obstacles in the old structure. Through prayers and with God's grace we were able to overcome all of them.

The general contractor's name was Tommy Wolfe, a godsend. He was smart, courteous, and a professional in his conduct with me and the leadership. I had had experience working with many contractors, but with Tommy, I could not have found better. He knew how to navigate out of troubling situations with concrete solutions, which made my job managing the project easier. It was if he was born to do the job.

Eleven months from the start and two months overdue, I was able to sign off on the completed renovations. It was absolutely breathtaking and all worth it at the end to watch the parishioners as they walked in to see their beautiful sanctuary on Mother's Day in 1996. The church was designed to seat almost five hundred parishioners. The choir loft sat over eighty. The rear of the choir loft was designed with three windows. A large window in the center flanked by two smaller windows viewed the Tappan Zee Bridge spanning the Hudson River. The sanctuary was jam-packed on most Sunday mornings. I had included in the renovation closed circuit televisions in the dining room. This accommodated the overflow of parishioners who couldn't find a seat in the sanctuary.

Offerings were doing very well at that time. We were able to pay down the loan we took from the M&T Bank within three years, instead of seven. The reason I pushed to pay off the loan was obvious. If we had not paid the loan within seven years, the church would have had to refinance the remaining balance, costing additional interest and administrative expenses. Even with cost overruns, the construction project left the Tabernacle Church with no deficits and a substantial amount of cash on hand.

COUNTED ON

After the construction was completed, I revisited the issue of the missing church funds with Trustee Tessy. Tessy is the same board member that sat across from me at mom's dining room table at the first meeting. She was slightly heavyset with swollen ankles that appeared to pain her when she stood or shuffled in her half-heel black shoes. Her shoes looked to be undersized for her puffy feet as they leaned to the outer edges.

Tessy had mastered the image of someone who was barely making it by dragging her feet. She carried an aura that solicited unconscious sympathy. She had a tooth missing that caused her to cover her mouth with her left hand when she smiled or laughed. She had a habit of saying, "You know, you know." She appeared to be quiet, speaking in a whisper where you could barely hear her. The same way Tessy conducted herself with a mystical behavior shrouded in secrecy, she conducted the church business in the darkness of night with little to no transparency to congregants. Tessy cleared her name from the funds debacle when she told me she knew who was taking the church monies. She said, "I was praying for God to show the pastor what was going on." She went on telling me she was very close to leaving the church. Standing up in front of her desk, Tessy walked over to the office door, placing her right hand on the doorknob. She then turned her body slightly so I could observe her right hand on the knob. Tessy said to me, "That is just how close I was to leaving the church. I'm telling you. You know, you know." She went on to say she knew what the head trustee was doing and how much he was taking.

I nodded my head slightly as I listened to her testament. Placing an empty chair in front of the combination safe in the trustee office, she said she would often find it there when she arrived at the office. Tessy chuckled as she said, "He would leave the chair sitting in front of the safe after he left." When she finished, I asked her why she had not informed my mother as to what was going on. She responded with a blank stare through her black framed glasses. So I asked her again. Tessy, looking perplexed, after a long pause said, "The pastor wouldn't have believed me anyhow. Pastor is very fond of the head deacon and his wife."

I said to Tessy, "I can't believe that you allowed pilferage to go on and not say something to my mother about it." I was giving the same look she gave me earlier as I said "Okay, I'll see you later" and walked out of the trustee office door.

I went to my mother and asked her what kind of reporting she was getting from the trustees. Mom replied, "I was being told each Sunday by the head deacon and head trustee (who is the same person), 'Pastor, the offering was up a little from last Sunday' or 'Pastor the offering was down a little from the Sunday before.' Here I am thinking that things are going along all right, and we are about to be put out on the street." When I took the position, I ensured that mom received a weekly verbal and written account of all funds. My sister and I trained the trustees on how to fill in spreadsheets along with other forms of information that mom could have at her fingertips (e.g., number of attendees at every service, exact dollar amounts of offerings taken up). I moved through the church organization, discovering the church had soft areas left unprotected with no accountability when handling funds. The church was operating a small retail store that also sold VHS tapes, DVDs, and CDs. I found shrinkage in the inventory from the store. I decided to clamp down when I saw a sister working the store with her open pocketbook sitting next to the cash register. I closed the church store by placing most of the merchandise into vending machines in the dining hall. The vending machines paid for themselves in less than two years.

The church had been leasing a water fountain that I returned at the end of the lease agreement and purchased a new drinking fountain. I was able to save the church additional funds by focusing my attention on other leased equipment that was underutilized. Meanwhile, I continued the church's marketing campaign for new membership by installing a membership committee. We set up a church organizational responsibility chart and appointed an active community outreach coordinator. Mom said to me that she had never had the church run so smoothly before, and she felt less pressure and burden by having things being well managed. I consider myself an anointed strategist and manager of organization and accountability.

It is unfortunate some people do not like order, and they keep things in chaos and confusion to hide their agendas or weaknesses. There are times that a truth and a lie can look identical, challenged by confusion to clarify the two. However, confusion is good. Confusion allows you the opportunities to sort things out, bringing clarity to situations. I have learned from church and corporate America to not underestimate what people can do to create chaos and disrupt order. A person with poor intentions will often find biblical scriptures to back up their bad behaviors. They will even go as far as saying God told them to say or do what they are doing or did. I am not a theologian; however, I do understand certain passage of scripture from a spiritual aspect and fundamental religious order.

As the church membership grew, I continued doing what I could to help Mother. Things were coming together as I carefully monitored church funds. With mom's direction I installed policies and procedures, along with the latest computer technology programs that enhanced the business of the church. The policies and desktop programs were great checks and balances for everyone. The trustee board wrote job descriptions that were comprehensible for department heads. Having regular business meetings gave more transparency to the membership. Implementing organizational charts with a clear view of who was responsible for what was also helpful.

After about a year of meetings with the ministerial board of the church, I started to get low-level resistance from several people who said God had called them to preach. They were all ordained ministers of the church. Within four years of my return and hard work, I could feel an undercurrent from about five or six of the ministers. I had set a few things in order over the years. Unfortunately, putting things correct and in order will sometimes inflame people. Earlier, I discovered one of the church ministers had a drug abuse problem. Minister Sy was a soft-spoken gentleman, personable, with a bright wide smile, who wore a gold chain around his neck with a cross attached. He was accommodating, respectful, and formidable with church members. Minister Sy was excellent at getting the worshippers excited, up on their feet, hands waving, with an abundance of "amen" support from the congregation. However, I discovered Minister Sy was using crack cocaine.

How I stumbled onto this was eye-opening. We had a small number of members who were students at the Manhattan Bible Institute. Each week the church provided transportation into New York City for their classes. Minister Sy was assigned to the transport department and volunteered to shuttle the students with one of two of the church's fifteen-passenger vans. First, I learned that on at least two occasions Minister Sy was up to two hours late picking up the students. Then one evening he returned the van with a window broken. While he gave an eloquent explanation, it was unconvincing to both me and the other trustee board members. My suspicions grew when he failed to retrieve the Manhattan Bible College students on another occasion. In each instance, we lost track of where he could have been on those evenings.

When I met with him about his disappearances, I noticed symptoms that were pointing to possible drug abuse. Part of my corporate training included identifying drug use in the workplace. Initially he denied any drug use, but with the assurance of help he admitted being hooked on crack cocaine. My mom, along with two other ministers, immediately responded, and arrangements were made for him to enter a program located in Pomona, New York. After his drug treatment program, Sy relocated to the Midwest. It was at this point that I began to peel away the veneer of people's agendas. As things were unfolding, I noticed Ministers Sy and Lesley gave the impression to be especially close with each other.

Mom, over the years, would look at me over the top of her reading glasses saying in an intense monotone voice, "Now you take Lesley, he has my spirit." When Minister Lesley was out of Mom's eyesight, the congregants did not take him seriously. Lesley, as talented as he was, would do silly childlike things. For instance, one Wednesday evening during choir rehearsal he interrupted the rehearsal for a short while. My understanding is that on the downbeat of a song the choir broke out in intense laughter. The choir director, standing with her back to the double doors, turned to see why everyone was so amused. With her hands in the air, she saw Minister Lesley garbed in his hospital scrubs and white sneakers somersaulting down the center aisle to the altar. Minister Lesley was known for showing up to the Tabernacle Church and other churches in his scrubs. He would sing at funerals, running in quickly, giving his condolences on behalf of his pastor and the Tabernacle Church family, telling everyone he had to get back to work.

One day I asked mom if she thought Les was gay. She replied, "I think he has had an encounter." Mom continued by saying, "If he were not in the Tabernacle Church, Les would have been something else." I left it at that, for you see I have friends in law enforcement who told me that they came upon a vehicle with two gentlemen in the car with their pants down. By their descriptions, I was later able to identify the two people as Ministers Sy and Lesley.

I continued working to smooth out the church business and make sense of the organization. Among things, I wanted to ensure we had a copy of a valid driver's license for all people driving church vans or the pastor's vehicle in case of an accident or other emergency. During the course of a Transportation Department meeting, I asked them to make their driver's license available so we could make copies for the church files. Out of five drivers, only one had a valid driver's license, with the exception of Minister Les who had a learner's permit. How was he driving the pastor to Brooklyn and across the George Washington Bridge when drivers with learner's permits are not allowed to drive over the bridges?

On one particular occasion the church sponsored a revival where the offerings collected were over seven thousand dollars. I got into a conflict with mom and Tessy over compensating the minister that preached during the revival with five thousand dollars. Their argument was they wanted her to come back. Some years later that same preacher, mom, and the leadership regime encountered some type of discord between them, resulting in a permanent riff. After that I started having ministers sign off on the money the church was putting in their pockets, reporting that amount to the IRS using a 1099 form. What a problem that created. Ministers don't want to pay income tax on their offerings or gifts. One minister told me that they could not see giving that much money to the government.

During the summer of 1996, the church leadership regime paid bail to free a sex offender from the county jail. The person was the choir vice president who was a bounce-around person going from church to church representing the Tabernacle Church with his singing talent. He was arrested for inappropriate behavior with a minor. When the incident took place, he was employed at the St. Agatha Home for Children in Nanuet, New York. The Clarkstown Police Department made the arrest, holding him for a substantial bail. I recommended the church use a reputable bail bondsman by the name of George Garmon. I didn't want to dip into the church treasury for his bail. Instead, the church could collect money from individuals. Against my advice, Tessy and the inner circle convinced mom to use church funds to bail the popular church songster from the county jail.

On Sunday mornings, he would direct the Tabernacle choir while leading the devotional worship service. Each service he wore a different-colored hand towel loosely around his neck as he led the choir in song. The color of the hand towel around his neck blended nicely with the color of his suit for the day. Midway through a song he would begin to lightly blot away the perspiration from his forehead, face, and neck with the towel.

The choir vice president held another secret. He was apprehensive and absolute about not announcing his preference to be with a same gender-sex partner. In the past he was able to maintain his secret by staying in the closet about his behavior. He knew mom and the church leadership regime would respond negatively if he were to publicly announce his beliefs on same-sex union. He felt that announcing his sexual preferences would jeopardize his position to continue leading the choir and devotional services. He had served as the choir vice president to mom for several years. After his public record of arrest, mom was forced to uphold the church doctrine, silencing him for an extended time. After six months he was allowed to resume his responsibility as the choir vice president. Despite his arrest he was persistent in carrying forward his inappropriate behavior with minors.

I continued to move forward holding the ministerial board accountable to the church ministry and the vision of my mother despite the resistance of a few. The ministerial board had eighteen ministers ordained by mother. Six of the ministers had great weight upon who was allowed in their circle as they controlled the direction of the church. I called this group the inner circle six because they were extremely influential on mother's decisions. This resistance of the inner circle six was persistent, even in the wake of weekly meetings where everyone could have a voice. Suddenly ministers started not showing up to scheduled meetings they had committed themselves. I had one minister's wife ask if I would excuse her husband from a one-hour meeting after a church service to go shopping. I had left the ministerial board to be the last folks to work with thinking they would be the most secured group. In the days ahead the ministerial board proved to be the most difficult department of the church.

The resistance steadily grew in the inner circle six. They certainly did not want to be held accountable. I was interfering with their comfort zone. The subtleties started with verbal and distinct assaults on my character. The one rumor that I remember most was that I was trying to take over the church from my mother. The more I held the inner six accountable, the more difficult things became for me. It created a riff between mom and me.

The discord between my mother and I became severe when mom actually believed the inner circle six's insistence that I was trying to take over her church. Keep in mind, I am not an ordained minister or proclaimed by God to be anything. I was invited to the church to help. Just when I thought the allegations would blow over and mom would come to her real senses, it became worst. The attacks and allegations continued from the pulpit. One of the inner circle six, wearing a gold cross and backward collar, preached a sermon about business in the church. He told the parishioners, "God's church don't need *no* business in his house. This church is run by the Holy Ghost. Take that stuff somewhere else."

Mom sat in her large white chair positioned on a six-inch riser on her pulpit, nodding her head in a large white hat, saying, "Amen." Trying to hang in there, I met with mom at home. While we discussed certain issues, the last words from her were, "God did not tell me that I was to let you organize my church." She asked me to step down from my position while she stood eating an orange at the kitchen island.

COUNTED OUT

AT THE NEXT MINISTERIAL BOARD meeting I announced my resignation to the board. Most were in disbelief. I could see and feel the relief from the inner circle six that created this situation. One of the outer circle ministers stood up saying, "I don't believe this is what God wants." From that moment, mother operated secretly, launching a platform from her pulpit to discredit her children and anyone who got in her way. She used her psychology and power of pastoral care to fling herself into a position of "poor me." The leadership regime, led by the inner circle six, encouraged her to pastor her church from a pedestal.

The dichotomy within mom's church and her undying efforts paid off. The proof was in the sympathy she garnered, the respect she demanded, and the adornment from scores of folks. Mom would often say to me, "You don't know who I am!" When she said this, I always gave the same response, "You're Maw..." The problem mom is facing now is her skills have become dull. She is not as skillful as she once was in pulling things off without a glitch. Mom has become haphazard with people, which causes them to get angry and leave the Tabernacle Church. Her attitude would show through when she would say, "I don't care if they do leave, they ain't nobody!" As I started down the aisle to leave the sanctuary where the meeting was held, mom called me back. I politely answered, and as I walked back, she looked at me and decreed, "It is appropriate." I nodded my head, turned, and walked down the aisle, making my way through the double doors. Confused and numb, I collected my belongings while trying to sort out in my mind what this was all about. I sent out memos to all the department heads with the news of mom asking me to step down. It sent shock waves through the church organization. I told the department heads to compare the situation they were about to enter into with the history of Moses in the dessert for forty years, and I didn't have it in me to sit around and watch. I offered my help in any way if they ever needed me. I was a phone call away.

When my sister and I left the organization, the membership had no closure as to why we were leaving. The situation remained a mystery to the organization's membership with plenty of gossip and rumors. I underestimated the inner circle six's leadership regime on how ingrained, inbred, and powerful they were. They were able to divide and conquer their pastor and her family. Where others would be apprehensive to tell mom the truth, her family would. One of the characteristics of family love is honesty with each other, and a feeling of emotional safety.

At some point mom asked me for my opinion as to why I thought a close friend of our family and prominent doctor didn't join her church. She distinctively focused on the late Dr. Fletcher Johnson who was at one time one of the best cardiovascular thoracic surgeons on the East Coast. Mom often told me how she was tired of preaching to the same people all the time.

Dr. Johnson was a close friend despite his personal challenges in the latter years of his career. Dr. Johnson was a great physician right up until his death in 2009. I responded to Mom's question with an honest answer. I said, "Not only Dr. Johnson but also your church should have many professional members. Your congregation should have a mixture of people. Professionals not only bring their skills and talents but tithe and offerings as well." What Tessy and the inner circle continued to tell Mom during and after the mass exodus of people was, "There was too much God in the Tabernacle for the believers and nonbelievers." I always felt Mom had a ministry that drew a diverse range of worshipers. Mom's ministry seemed to lean toward all walks of life. I remember frequent prophecies, saying that Mom's ministry claimed the entire county. I sincerely believed that.

However, Tessy and the inner circle leadership stifled the ministry growth by maintaining a choke hold on the church. The inner circle, fueled by jealousy and an ambitious zeal to garner attention from mom, capped the ministry with incompetence, placing limitations on talented people in the church. Tessy and the inner circle allowed mom to think she had to be the president over every auxiliary in her church. Tessy, who was the head trustee board member, never called for church business meetings. Mom, being the chief executive officer of her organization, was not privy to sound advice from Tessy and the inner circle. Tessy and the inner circle fell way short of supporting mom as the visionary.

When I was engaged with the church organization, I spoke frankly and openly about maintaining the core membership while improving upon the professionalism of the church experience. The inner circle made Mom feel threatened by smart or educated people around her. I use the word *educated* not so much in terms of grade point average or college degrees earned. I am making inference to *smart people*. Smart is what smart does. I offered mom and the inner circle things the church could do (e.g., book clubs, writer's club, career seminars, music clubs, accredited college courses, professional counseling services, outreach programs—last, but not least, business plans with clear and crisp objectives taken directly from mom's vision).

Mom's church had a family member for every generation with my sister, our younger brother, and my three nephews. My sister, brother, oldest nephew, and I were all working professionals. My other two nephews were attending school. My sister is a talented songstress and director, among many other talents. She was responsible for putting the Tabernacle Church choir together. My oldest nephew is gifted and talented. He is an excellent organist and music producer. He has his own radio show on a popular FM station in New York City. He was recently awarded with the best radio show by the Underground Academy Awards. He has produced and worked with music greats: Beyoncé

Knowles, Mariah Carey, Donna Summers, and Kelly Rowlings, along with producing many shows on the FM radio station where he works.

He was the church organist and minister of music for a number of years until the church leadership regime started picking at him. They wanted him to choose between what they called God's music and the devil's music. After the leadership regime created a buildup and a string of discord between mom and her grandson, they stood back and watched the scene unfold. Their efforts culminated after a Sunday worship service when one of the inner circle six pointed out to mom three water bottles and debris in the musician's area and some small scratches on the Hammond organ. One thing led to another, and mayhem ensued when mom slammed one of my nephew's keyboards and other equipment to the sanctuary floor.

Around this time, I was married to Pauline. She was my junior high school childhood sweetheart and puppy love who, years later by sheer coincidence, I ran into in a Marshall's department store parking lot in Nanuet, New York. Pauline was my first and only marriage. Pauline had been married twice and was divorced from her second husband when we caught up with each other. I was in my late thirties. Pauline had two adult children, Vanessa who was very attractive and Bobby who was handsome and who Pauline adored. Vanessa was the mother of two small children, a three-year-old and a one-year-old. Pauline held intense feelings and unconditional love for her children and grandchildren. If any of Pauline's children's name came up in conversation, Pauline would light up with a wide smile, glowing with pride.

After sparking and courting for six months, I asked Pauline to marry me. Pauline became a member of the church instantly. Mom encouraged Pauline to join the sound and video department, which she did, and later mom placed her on the trustee board. Over the years I noticed how Tessy and Pauline's relationship drew very close. They would whisper secrets to each other in the office and giggle with each other most of the time. Pauline would call Tessy Lou as a nickname. I never stopped to ask them why Pauline was calling her Lou. Pauline did have a habit of nicknaming her closest of friends.

One particular Sunday morning I conducted a meeting with the sound and video department. This meeting initiated the need to place professional labels on all VHS tapes, DVDs, DVs, and cassette tapes using a desktop program. While I was speaking, my wife blurted out, "I don't know why we have to listen to you and your ideas." She continued to disapprove of my suggestions during the meeting. I had never encountered Pauline speaking with such a provocative, incensed tone, let alone in front of other people. Something wasn't right with her.

By 2001, my marriage to Pauline was dissolving. I elected to temporarily leave my house because Pauline and her lawyer, Ms. Gargotta, had filed a motion barring our cohabitating in the same house. In addition, my mother and I disagreed on Pauline's divorce proceedings against me. Through all of this we all continued to attend the same church.

My attorney was an eighty-four-year-old retired English professor prior to practicing law by the name of Alan Wolk. Always speaking with a soft, deliberate tone, he appeared to be somewhat of an eccentric. He was a man with strong core values, honesty being foundation of his most esteemed beliefs. Often his wisdom came into view from his quiet veneer. Alan reminded me of the late Peter Fauk who starred as a police detective named Colombo. Detective Colombo's famous line was, "Just one more thing." Although Alan never made the quote, I often anticipated that he would. Alan started out as our lawyer. He became my lawyer through default.

After Pauline agreed with the settlement agreement, I hired Alan to draw it up and file at the county courthouse within thirty days under irreconcilable differences. Under the terms of the agreement we would split our joint bank account and she would be awarded 50 percent of my two personal accounts. It felt fair as Pauline had entered the marriage with no real assets and she retained her entire salary throughout our fourteen years together. When we divorced, she was earning approximately $68,000 per year. Pauline would be leaving the marriage in a better financial condition than she came. The divorce started out to be amicable and uncontested. We both agreed to use Alan to draw up the final settlement. After it was mutually signed, Pauline's boyfriend decided differently. It was not enough. He wanted the house. Without notice she retained the legal services of one Ms. Gargotta, who promised her the world and my head on a platter.

Ms. Gargotta and Pauline filed a motion that accused me of assaulting her in front of Alan at his office as I forced her to sign the divorce agreement. Ms. Gargotta had arrived from nowhere, wasting no time posturing herself. She was gruff with this wild, frizzy, unruly hair seeming to sprout from her head. She did not come with a wagonload of manners. She was a tough-talking attorney with an aggressive, hateful attitude, flexing her muscles. While I felt it all to be unnecessary, Alan said he was not surprised, that he had seen this over and over again. It was about how much pain could be distributed from one person to another. Alan said to me, "Ms. Gargotta is mostly a homemaker with small children. She runs home between court proceedings to change diapers. She has never won a case in her career." Alan went on to say, "Ms. Gargotta makes promises to her clients that she can't fulfill. Whether she loses or wins, she still gets paid. Can't you talk with your wife before this gets too far gone." My reply to Alan was, "I'll try."

The next day Ms. Gargotta petitioned the court to depose Mr. Wolk as a witness on their allegation I beat Pauline up and forced her to sign the settlement agreement. Alan was livid! Alan said in his mannerism, "Pauline is lying again. You really married out of your class."

Ms. Gargotta was attempting to transpose Alan into a witness so he could no longer represent me and to drive the litigation cost of the civil suit higher. The judge dismissed the motion after Alan's response to the court concerning Ms. Gargotta and Pauline's allegations. One day in his office Alan said to me, "I understand that you all have a beautiful home up in Stony Point." He continued with, "Ms. Gargotta says that it's absolutely lovely."

I incredulously asked Alan, "How does she know that?" Alan said, "Pauline invited her to meet with your mother at the house." Alan went on to say, "I would love for you to invite me up sometimes to see it." I just stood with my mouth open, looking stunned. I said, "Alan, are you telling me that Pauline had her attorney inside our home?" Alan began to describe what Ms. Gargotta saw inside the house to a T. Now I understood why mom was sitting on the opposite side of me in the courtroom with Pauline and Ms. Gargotta.

On one of our court days, over a year into court proceeding, my sister and I grabbed a bite to eat at the end of the session. On our way home I drove up Main Street in New City, New York. Ms. Gargotta's office is on the same Street. As I drove past, my sister said, "Ale," which is my nickname. "Look! Mom is coming from Gargotta's office!" I said, "What," as I turned my head to glance. My sister was livid. I couldn't believe it. I felt anger and disappointment. I was almost on the verge of tears. It was as if someone punched me in my gut. Mom never saw us going by her as she exited from Ms. Gargotta's office door. During the next court proceeding, Ms. Gargotta started arguing with Alan in the hallway as to whose witness Mom was. Mom stood there not saying a word while Alan told Ms. Gargotta that the mother is with the son.

She said, "No, the mother is my witness."

Alan turned to mom and started lecturing her on the fact that she was our witness. Alan said to mom, "This is your son. I have a daughter-in-law that I love dearly, but if it comes to my son and my daughter-in-law, I stick with my kid." Mom was unresponsive to Alan. I felt abandoned and let down. I drove away from the court thinking about how could rest at night or minister to families. Family values are if your child is having trouble, you defend them without question, without reservation, and without choice. Parents in the church were in disagreement with mom over this valued principle, except for Lesley. However, they dared not openly disagree with her antics. When it came to their children, they just quietly and selectively disobeyed her.

I have observed mom stand in the pulpit telling her congregants that friendship should only last about seven years. Mom believed that if something should happen to the begotten children, the grandparents should not and were not to raise their grandchildren. She said, "God did not create parents to raise a second set of children." Mom over the years has made known her posture to be antifamily and nonprincipled in family value.

LOVE AND FORGIVE

AFTER ALL WAS SAID AND done at the end of an almost two-year process, the original divorce agreement stood on its own merit. On the final day of court as the judge read the decision, Pauline stood with her attorney weeping uncontrollably. When the judge finished, he asked her if she wanted to say anything. Sobbing, she said, "I don't know what happened, things just fell apart. I didn't think it would get this far. My life is over." When the judge asked me if I had anything to say, I said, "Your honor, I have but one request. I would like for my ex-wife to change her name back to her maiden name." That was the last time I saw my ex-wife. Our marriage was dissolved in 2002. That was then and this is now. After the divorce case ended, I asked my mother why she bankrolled Pauline's civil suit against me. Mom simply brushed it away by saying, "Pauline is a liar." Over the years and with many therapy sessions, I have come to learn that some scars can last for a lifetime. However, time heals the deepest of scars and mends shattered hearts.

Meanwhile, after a great deal of pressure from mom, my brother agreed to their prearranged living agreement. He uprooted himself, leaving his home in Virginia to return home. He had earned his master's degree in communications and public relations from Regent University in Virginia Beach, Virginia.

Mom and I had purchased a house in 1999 with close to four thousand square feet of living space, more than sufficient for two people.

Through the years my career required I work in several states. Looking back, from time to time mom would call to tell me my siblings were not treating her well. She would ramp me up to the point I would call my siblings telling them to stop treating mom poorly. I was never sure what they had done to mom, if anything. Sometimes they said nothing, and at other times they would say they didn't know what I was talking about. Truth be told, neither did I. When my brother arrived back home, he was instrumental in getting a scene shot at the church for *The Manchurian Man* starring Denzel Washington. While the scenes did not make it into the movie, the church and the people used in the shot were paid well.

Somewhere into the second year of my brother and mother's living arrangement, their relationship started to go down. The church leadership regime for whatever reason did not like my brother interfering and being at the church. Once again, the inner circle planted and nourished a seed of division between mom and her youngest son.

During a severe snowstorm in January 2004, I received a frantic telephone call at 3:30 a.m. from my sister. I could hear the agitation in her voice. She said, "Mom put Steven out of the house a little while ago in this storm." Shaking myself awake, I said, "What did you say?" When she repeated what she had said, I could feel and hear how disturbed and upset she was.

Dosie and Janine were the primary players in this mean-spirited plot against my brother. Dosie was mom's head nurse. Her primary duty was to make sure mom wanted for nothing. She assisted her in getting baths, picking out clothing, carrying bags, going on vacations, running errands, and sometimes assisting with light cleaning. Janine was a member of mom's church who lived in Amityville Long Island. Working with Dosie, she conspired with mom to remove my brother from the house. This came on the heels of my brother not agreeing with some of Mom's antics and doctrines in the church. Compelled by his convictions, he spoke straightforwardly to mom and the inner circle about certain practices within the church that bothered him. With that information the inner circle went to work. I remembered in early years hearing Reverend Helen tell mom, "Don't get your hands dirty." Influenced by Dosie and Janine, mom got an order of protection against her son, falsely accusing him of hitting her. As Steven remembers the events leading up to his unlawful eviction, Janine and Dosie were in the house for over two days as he came and went. He was unsuspecting, just noticing they were continually whispering together during the day and early parts of the evening. My brother said they directed big smiles toward him, acting like junior high school girls sharing secrets with each other. He did notice that mom stayed in her bedroom, which was unusual.

At three in the morning, my brother was awaked by Janine's voice. She was calling him from the bottom of the stairs in the foyer where both she and Dosie stood. Janine said in a sluggardly condescending tone, "Stevennn, there's someone here to see you." He came from his room to the top of the staircase, and there looking up at him were six deputy sheriffs. One of the sheriffs asked if he was Steven Alston. He responded with "Yes, that's me." The deputy sheriff held up a court order, saying, "You will have to vacate the premises immediately. You have a standing order of protection filed against you."

Days later, once the storm lifted I drove over five hundred miles to see about our brother. As I approached him, I saw tears well up in his eyes as I listened to him, his voice quivering. I could not help but notice as I listened to his side of the story how heartbroken he was. He couldn't hide his feelings.

The pain I saw on his face was unforgettable. My brother had been humiliated, thrown out of the house in the middle of a winter snowstorm. A direct attack on his well-being by incensed church people. After all this, Janine began to slack off, making herself scarce. She had been an active member for over twenty-five years, serving as one of mom's nurses, but her attendance at church services were noticeably less. Her excuse was that the church was too far for her to travel.

Recently I spoke with my brother Steven about what happened nine years ago on the day of his unlawful eviction by mom. In his account, he makes mention of allegations mom made against me. Here are his words:

I was thinking about the order of protection mom wrote against me. It was all untrue. Mom would go in, snoop around in my room when I was not there. I came home one day, and as I was leaving and about to lock the door, she came around the corner pushing and hitting me because she wanted to get into my room. Mom reported to the police that I hit her and then wrote up an order of protection against me. Not only that, she spread that falsehood to everyone in her church and the county. People had become cold to me because they couldn't understand how I could get so angry as to hit my mother.

But I thank God that my youngest nephew, Brandon, was in the house at the time and witnessed it all. Brandon testified that I did not hit her and it was not true. He said, "Nana attacked my uncle and started hitting him." I'm so glad that Brandon was there. This could have affected the opportunity given to me to work for the New York State Department of Labor, which served to be the most important career move of my life. In both instances this was a clever and evil plan, a method to destroy her children's reputations. Mom made this assault and character assassination attempt on both of us, which truly and clearly identified her main goal, to destroy. The Bible says, "The devil comes to kill steal and destroy." I truly believe that her accusations of you and me are being ruled by the enemy. Mom has been used by the spirit of evil thoughts against us. I am thankful to say it didn't work and you and I don't have any blemishes on our records. Thanks be to God! Now I know that you as well as I, truly, without question, *love* and *forgive* our mother.

I feel led in my heart that we must use wisdom and our experiences to identify and deal with these types of issues and problems to help others not to suffer reputation damage. When you look beyond the obvious, there is a purpose and lesson related to what we've endured so far. Actions taken by family members who we trust, love, care for, and look out for sometimes can deeply hurt us, bringing on untold pain. I still yet remain confused by mom's actions. Her unwarranted actions and behaviors have not changed my prayers for her or my unconditional love that I hold for her.

Steven encountered and was subjected to the same privacy issues and personal violations I faced prior to my departure. Although my bedroom was never locked, mom would open every piece of mail and each parcel that was addressed to me. Then she would write across the face of the envelope, "Sorry. Opened by mistake." There were times the envelopes came from my company headquarters with employee personal information enclosed (e.g., salary history and wage information). Nothing stopped her, even when the mail was marked Confidential. The church's inner circle continued to paint the three of us as villainous to our mother. Mother started saying her children were against her and trying to take over her church. I viewed these actions and behavior of the inner circle as mean-spirited as it placed mom in a defensive mode against her children. I thought of this scripture as I watched how things were unfolding.

> Fathers, do not provoke or irritate or fret your children [do not be hard on them or harass them], lest they become discouraged and sullen and morose and feel inferior and frustrated. [Do not break their spirit.] (Colossians 3:2 Amplified Bible)

The scripture I heard all my life from the old testament was "Honor your father and your mother, so that you may live long in the land the Lord your God is giving you" (Exodus 20:12 NIV). My upbringing avoided the Colossians 3:2 passage.

Based on my experiences, I would recommend that pastors not just rely on loyalty alone and yes-men for their inner circles. Interview people thoroughly and check their backgrounds before you place them in positions of power to represent your organization. With so many church start-ups and church pop-ups, church corporate leadership regimes can easily originate out of cronyism and legalistic policies. These types of leadership regimes will not present a positive challenge to their minister. Positive respectful challenge is not a negative thing. It helps a pastor clearly view things more concisely with a better understanding of the situations at hand, provided you have the right people around you holding up your ladder—simply put, people placed into sensitive positions behaving responsibly in the presence of others whether in church or not. I would further recommend that pastors rotate people in many of these organizational positions and not allow a person to think or feel a position of power is theirs forever.

There are three key positions I can identify within Tabernacle's corporate regime: the pastor's personal secretary or administrator, her nurse, and her adjutants. Assigned to the wrong people, these positions can be deadly to parishioners. The head nurses of mom through the years were female, all with similar personalities. Dosie and her predecessors were more mechanical than spiritual in their support of her. The head nurse is not usually a registered professional nurse. This person serves as if they were a genie in a bottle: your request is my command. The position sometimes is much like a sentry where the nurse stands outside or inside the doorway as a guard and servant 24-7. The nurse steers people away from the pastor based on their own perceptions or decisions as to who should have access to the pastor. I have seen people wait several hours to see my mom. Now bear in mind she had already given instructions that she did not want to see a certain person, leaving them to wait. Eventually exhaustion or time would force them to leave. Nurses that I have known were demonstrative in their quest to control parishioners and to be out front in the limelight with mother. Mom's nurses rarely missed seizing opportunities to utilize written or unwritten rules to demonstrate their authority over congregants.

Dosie, who was mom's personal nurse and the head of the nursing department, held the position for years. She started the position when she was in her early thirties and is now in her fifties. Most of the time Dosie wore a cross or some other Christian symbol associated with God. However, she always had a stone-faced appearance, not welcoming to those around her. I believe her behavior is a result of a broken home coupled with poverty in childhood.

I recall mom yelling at Dosie often because she was thoughtless. Once she left mom's laptop at the Hartsfield-Jackson Atlanta airport. This was after mom reminded her several times to "be sure you have my laptop before we board the plane." On another occasion Dosie took two of my mother's expensive watches to be repaired at Zale's jewelry store in the Palisades Mall Center. The Zale's repair department called my mother, a year later, reminding her she had two watches that had not been picked up. Dosie said to my mother, "I lost the receipt and forgot about the watches." Dosie rarely wrote down any notes to keep her and the pastor organized. On many occasions Dosie would forget to pack my mother's shoes and other items she needed for preaching. Mom said she spent more time watching over Dosie than Dosie looking after her. Mom would often complain about how Dosie would outdress her in big church events such as her anniversary day or what she called "my day."

For years she acted as if she was computer illiterate by not knowing how to power up a computer even though she owned a laptop. Mom told me when she took Dosie to Aruba on vacations she would bring her own laptop. As mom regaled me with the stories about Dosie's computer illiteracy, I struggled to believe as mom did. I felt Dosie was being insincere about not knowing how to turn on her computer and using it. I really believed she was pulling the wool over her pastor's eyes. This gave Dosie a feeling of endearment and entitlement to our mother. Her pretense allowed Mother to feel more superior while she looked like the poor, submissive soul needing rescue. Her moods for attention changed daily, and she could be testy.

She seemed to always have an ACE bandage on her body someplace. She sometimes wore a cervical collar around her neck or used some other medical device. Dosie never seemed to be without some kind of bodily injury. It appeared Dosie's injuries were gimmicky to squeeze time from her job while going off on lavish vacations to Aruba and other places with mom—at the expense of the congregation. Dosie being the head of the nurse's aide department never gave any of the other members the opportunity to travel with their pastor. The department members would often complain about how unfair and thoughtless Dosie treated them. Dosie would demand the ladies under her supervision stay behind to care for her own mother who was sickly and an invalid while she travelled the world with mom. The other nurses would get into conflicts over this unfairness, and mom would subtly side with Dosie to shut them up.

Another most feared group of people are adjutants, who can be described as having chameleon personalities. Adjutants can come off as smiley, friendly, unfriendly, or militant. They stand around the hallways, mingling with the crowds, listening to conversations, then reporting what they overhear to the pastor and the church inner circle leadership regime. Minister Lesley was infamous for this behavior. The information they gather is usually laced with inaccuracies, based on hearsay, with conclusions drawn. Stories spun back to the pastor are intentionally subjective. Often remiss on facts, they incited poor judgment and would initiate harsh actions from Mother. I often wondered why the church leadership regime needed to eavesdrop on their membership and visitors.

The wisdom of my experience from working inside the church organization has led to a few suggestions we should be mindful of when building a church team. Church leadership means everyone must submit to Jesus and some form of human leadership. In a church corporate organization, no one should wield absolute, unquestionable authority. There should be a managed balance of power and authority through checks and balances. The strength of leadership must come from the Holy Spirit, not just a personality quiz over excessive cronyism. Often churches take money and pour it into incompetent staff. They should employ the best workers—people who are great at what they do and can mobilize others on God's mission. Make the hard calls when necessary with grace and courage. Honor Jesus's authority in your church as the senior pastor. When leaders are pushed outside of their capabilities, church health suffers. Leadership regimes should include a healthy combination of encouraging anecdotes, theology, and practical communications. Prophets, priests, paupers, and kings all exist in a congregation. Leadership should embrace the church body as they articulate their vision and mission.

I remember Pastor Cindy coming from Connecticut to preach on a regular basis at Tabernacle. She was a rather large woman who wore skintight dresses with low-cut V-necks showing her cleavage. Mom would privately and secretly complain to her inner circle about the way Cindy dressed but kept having her come back to preach. You see, Pastor Cindy awed the congregants with her many prophecies. In November 2000, she stood and told the congregation that a man was going to give the church a building for free before the end of December 2000. This prophecy took the congregation over the top as they went into mass hysteria—screaming, dancing, running around the church aisles, and waving their hands in the air. Now the only real estate developer and biggest name in the village was Joe Laguna. I had had several conversations with Joe. He was not going to give up any of his buildings for free. I had seen this dog and pony show many times over. The preacher flies into town announcing financial blessing for everybody. The only one getting the financial blessing is the preacher after he or she eloquently lifts it from your pockets and pocketbooks.

I find it quite amusing when I think back on those days. Most people are no more ahead today than when she arrived over ten years ago. I often wondered what happened. Did Pastor Cindy misinterpret what God said? Who was to blame for this blunder of a prophecy not coming to fruition? Could this prophecy have been the reason that forced mom and the inner circle to hastily purchase a building that was less than adequate in 2002?

Mom liked Cindy because she would beat up on the congregation telling them they weren't taking care of the pastor like they should. Pastor Cindy built her sermons on and around mom. Cindy was a pacifier to Mother while she was ostensibly acting for herself. Her offerings were between fifteen hundred and two thousand dollars per visit. Many churches give preachers a lot of money for preaching, or what I sometimes saw as a dog and pony show.

When my sister and I resigned our positions within the church corporation, we left it solvent, indebted to no one. The church had a liquid cash reserve of over three hundred thousand dollars. It seems, in the light of today, everybody is getting into the business of saving souls and opening churches. If one is a great motivational speaker, you can make a phenomenal living, with above-average pay, providing you find your audience.

SECOND TIME AROUND

AFTER MOM ASKED ME TO step down, my sister and I left the church on the same day, no choice of ours. On this day, my sister and I went to the trustee board office to say good-bye and wish everyone well. We chose not to go into any detail about the situation at hand. Three of the trustees were sincerely upset, not knowing what to say. Tessy played the role very well, as if she was going to cry. Later that day I called the trustee board to give them some pertinent information. I was disturbed when Tessy answered the phone with a bright hello and laughter, not knowing it was me and my sister on the other end. I had just left this lady appearing on the verge of tears, and now I could feel and hear her gleefulness coming through the phone at that moment. When she realized it was me, there was a moment of silence as she composed herself from the shock of hearing my voice. She then went into a solemn mode. I started to recall some things that went on with Tessy that at the time I treated as fleeting thoughts.

I flashed back to how she would get five hundred dollars from the church every time she had a death in her family. Tessy declared more mothers than I could count. She would claim this one and that one raised her, but these ladies that passed away were not her birth mother. She was giving herself honorariums throughout the year. The other thing I noticed, she would never go on vacations. She would sit at her desk for hours counting the same money and moving it around on her desk.

Tessy never made an effort to use the computer program software we had installed to the day I left. I happened to notice one day she had a black book with figures that she covered up quickly from my view. I asked her, "Are you running two sets of books?" As I thought of the inner six, Tessy was the sixth person, telling my mother I was taking over her church. In fact, she was working both me and my mother, always telling each what they wanted to hear. I noticed how mom protected Tessy. No one was allowed to say anything that would be perceived as negative toward her. Among the members, one of many complaints about her was not being reimbursed for authorized purchases. Those who had to deal with her usually came away frustrated and angry. Many times I had to diffuse unnecessary disputes by directing her to reimburse people their money. The Tabernacle Church lost several department heads because of Tessy. The trustee board operated under a cloak-and-dagger way of thinking. The inner circle six kept secrets within their circle and had mom's ear—what they said was law whether it is the truth or a lie.

I started to collect my thoughts as I thought about two loyal parishioners to mom's ministry. One lady against her husband's wishes wrote out a check for thirty thousand dollars after she took an early retirement payout from her company AT&T. She wrote another personal check to mom in the amount of seventeen thousand dollars. These checks never crossed my desk. I just happened to be going through bank statements and found these deposits. My wife would bring the money to the Nanuet National bank on Wednesdays for deposit. She never bothered to mention these special deposits made by Tessy and her. Eventually the inner circle six drove this member from the church, feeling threatened at the thought of her wanting to be the pastor.

The Tabernacle Church had another member that owned her business for years and was the largest giver and tithe payer. In her loyalty and love of the ministry, she was paying in tithe alone over thirteen thousand dollars per year. This member had a teenage daughter who would reluctantly attend Sunday services. The discord that ensued between the daughter and the inner circle could not be resolved. This was when Tessy and the inner circle banned the daughter from the church building. Needless to say, after seven years of affiliation, this member and mother left Tabernacle Church.

All three members had experienced a severe personal riff with the church leadership regime. They departed with broken hearts, and divided from their monies. As for the lady who left with her daughter, she was crying out for assistance and support being she was a single parent. I am most certain that one of the daughter's life experiences will be a grievance concerning church conduct. Two other parishioners who experienced their own painful exit from the church regaled me with one of their experiences. They were shopping for apparel in preparation for mom's yearly appreciation day held in October. Here is what they observed that day. "We went with Reverend Helen to New Jersey to look for dresses and shoes for the pastoral anniversary. We didn't find what we were looking for, however Reverend Helen saw something that she wanted to purchase. When we got to the register to pay, the reverend pulled out a tithe envelope from her bag, taking money out of it. When she noticed we saw her, she said, 'I'll put it back later.' I don't know if the money was put back or not. I do know the cash came from a tithe envelope with a parishioner's name written on it."

Church givers are busy people. Church corporate leadership regimes can serve all givers by ensuring money is used strategically and providing transparent accountability. Whether a large or small donor, a nonprofit church should not change the relationship and desire to serve and care for them. Church corporate regimes should value givers for more than just their financial contributions and gifts, but also for their passion, skills, and gifts that God has given them.

Several months after my sister and I left, the church leadership regime purchased a property for $637,000. The leadership regime used most of the reserve as a down payment and financed the balance. Because of the real estate markets trending downward, the church leadership overpaid for a building whose foundation had sank six inches. At the time unbeknownst to the leadership, the structure had extensive fire damage behind the sheet rock and a litany of other problems. The church leadership regime purchased the property with the intent to create an educational center, naming the building the Faith Educational and Community Center. After the regime found out that they were sold a lemon and since the property only had six parking spaces, the building was demolished. The corporate leadership regime allowed mom to walk right into this trap.

After nearly eight years of the project stalling and moving extremely slowly, in acute frustration mother contacted me for help. I answered her call with, "Yes, I will be glad to help in any way I can." I arrived on the scene in June 2009. I also had just released my first book and had already committed myself to book signing dates. My schedule was already hectic, but when mom called, I could not say no. I met with mom, Reverend Helen, promoted head trustee Tessy, and alternate trustee board member Deacon Loren. For the second time around, I found myself sitting at the dining room table in the month of June with these trustees.

Mom spoke on the frustration she was having with the construction. Mom said, "We need help. Tessy and I did not know how difficult this was going to get." I listened attentively to my mother while noticing the others around the table sat quietly. The three—Reverend Helen, Tessy, and Deacon Loren—had no input into this meeting. I continued to listen closely as I jotted down an action list for myself. When mom finished speaking, I started out with my initial thoughts. The building had been under construction with the same general contractor for almost eight years. I explained to mother and the others that I would start out with a written specific business plan. I asked several questions of the group and received halfhearted answers.

Two of the three pertinent questions were answered by Tessy: When is the deadline for the construction to be completed? She told me April 2010. How much money are you working with? "We don't have any money in the treasury." Can you give me names of a few volunteers to help me? They could not give me one name of a volunteer to help. I found that to be odd. I said to all of them that this was a difficult project. I continued with, "In my experience, projects range from 1 to 6 in difficulty levels. Using a level of difficulty with this project, it is definitely a 6." I took the time to explain to them and later to the full board of trustees the difficulty factors. I asked for a strong level of commitment on their part and full cooperation to get this project done.

My objective with prayer was to return back to them a full-functioning, viable community center within two to three years that would employ at least five or more paid workers with a bigger number of volunteers. After writing the plan, I requested a meeting with the full trustee board and mom. At this meeting I gave everyone a copy, and I reviewed each page.

I explained what essential paperwork was needed in order to finalize the business plan with completion dates as we move forward. I stated very clearly in the business plan that without paperwork, I would be unable to move forward when we reached a certain point. In addition, I explained that there was no charge for my time or work. With Mother's permission, I was able to initiate a meeting with some of the congregants. I requested volunteers, and with their support we were able to initiate a team of a diverse group of eight we called Team Project Representatives. I also drafted into the plan that I would become a lifelong trustee board member so as to ensure that situations like this would not happen again. The last page was a signature page that I asked the trustee board to sign off on, which they did. I was assured by Head Trustee Tessy that I would get the requested and needed paperwork promptly.

Mom installed me as pastor of church administration to oversee all business affairs of the church. This is where behaviors and things started to get dicey. Mom chose to make this announcement to her inner circle at a ministerial meeting combined with some of the trustee board members. On the back end of the meeting she said that it was her right to do this as the pastor. She concluded, "Some of you might not like this, but it is the right thing to do." She went on to say that she and Tessy could not handle this project. Tessy never agreed or disagreed with the pastor. I sat quietly watching their faces, focusing on Tessy's body language. While she did not vocalize her feelings, her body language spoke volumes about her discontent with mom's decision.

Three of the trustee board members said I was God sent, and they really needed me. One of the mothers of the church approached me in the hallway after a Sunday morning service and said, "I was wondering when these children are coming to help their mama." I gave her a smile and said, "I'm here."

Amazingly, the first Sunday I attended the morning worship service the sermon by one of the inner circle six was about Moses wandering around in the dessert for forty years. The spin was the parishioners were told that it was all right to wander around in the dessert because God allowed Moses and the Israelites to wander in the dessert. The minister went on to say that God will bring us out just like the Israelites.

The minister said, "They are laughing at us now, but when they see what God is going to do, we will have the last laugh." The minister said, "You don't know what God is going to do. God will send a millionaire through those doors and give the church a million dollars to help with the center. You don't know what God will do. I do know he will bring us out on top."

As I moved forward with the business plan, I started to run up against noncompliant behaviors from the inner circle six. Tessy promised me paperwork every week from late June through the end of September. The paperwork never came even after several verbal and written requests. The business plan called for the project to go into a holding pattern until the proper paperwork was satisfied. I estimated the cost to finish the second floor construction would hit an estimated one hundred thirty thousand dollars. The entire cost of this project was going to end conservatively at $1.2 million plus. That August I learned Tabernacle owed Phil, the general contractor, almost $80,000. I had been told at the onset of my involvement that the church did not owe Phil any money. Here is the memo I sent out to the board members in its entirety:

> Date: *August 11, 2009*
> Re: "The Faith Educational Community Center Community Development Corporation" (Faith Educational and Community Center)
>
> Message:
> Hello Everybody, Greeting in Christ our Lord and Savior. I trust that everyone is doing well. This is your bi-weekly update memo concerning where we are with the Center.
> Phil has delivered what I have requested of him on Tuesday August 4, 2009. Phil's invoices and paper work are neatly and professionally bound in

a binder with a cover sheet. His binder has indexes and cross references to everything he has done for the Church and the Faith Educational and Community Center, along with pictures. Phil has submitted his outstanding invoice, which shows two substantial amounts of money that we owe him. I am trying to get a handle on this amount with Tessy.

As of today I have very little paperwork from the church on our side of things. I have not finished my study on Phil's material; however our past behavior has been to pay him for the invoices and services that he has submitted, even though we are behind in payments according to Phil as of today.

There is nothing in his file indicating or documenting we have ever had a problem with his work or pricing, outside of the subcontractors that we brought in. I told Phil on August 4, 2009 that the day we felt we had to compete with his pricing and if we could not negotiate downward, "That's the day we should have fired you." After speaking with Phil and reviewing Phil's invoices the church paid him a substantial amount of money, so, Phil has decided to do what I call, "The 'right' thing." And that is to oblige the Church by extending service to fix certain items at the Center such as the air conditioning unit, and a few other punch list items. Phil says, we promised to pay him $5,000.00 per month until we pay him off on the current balance owed. Phil says he has not received regular payments since we asked for the agreement.

He also had me look at the checks he received that indicate we haven't honored our $5,000.00 per month arrangement with him.

This was the first I herd of this exact payment agreement. I do not have any further information about this arrangement with him. However, I took the liberty to renegotiate the payment from $5,000.00 to $3,000.00 per month. After much reluctance by Phil, he finally accepted the renegotiated payment of $3,000.00 per month. Although several years have pass since subcontractors have done work at the Center; I feel obligated to pursue reimbursements' for over payments for work and services.

For the rest of the work on the second floor of the Center I was premature, I went out and procured two contractors to bid on the job before we were ready to proceed, I also asked Phil for his bid. If I had more information about our finances I would have not have requested bids this early. The challenge we now face, contractors talk with each other. We have developed a reputation that we are slow to pay.

With the work that is left, some General Contractors don't see this as a viable project to keep subcontractors busy for any length of time, especially if we are competing against larger jobs that they might be bidding on. That coupled by the slow payments to Phil and placing him on a payment plan, leaves other Contractors a little unnerving about working for us. I continue to work at making the changes and adjustments that are needed to get us where we want to be and need to be.

Some of these changes and adjustments have been painful; however, it's been the right thing to do. I will continue to move and make the directions as clear as I possibly can. My work leads me to clean up the ambiguity in our church business department and get everyone onto the straight talk express.

I remind us all; this is about achieving the Pastor's Vision and meeting the Expectation. <u>Administrative Items needed since our first meeting in early June 2009</u>.

How much do we owe the General Contractor today?

What did we owe Phil in the first week of June 2009? Phil's original Bid for this job, along with other bids. Balance owed on The Faith Educational and Community Center?

How much (Cash) or liquid funds are available today?

Saving Accounts, Checking Accounts, or Cash? Mortgage Contracts Phil's original Contract.

Letter of Liens against the Church. All Deeds Bank Contracts, Bank Covenants What is Check Number 7593 for? What is Check Number 7745 for?

These items will allow me to cross reference Phil for accountability, and give us a handle on this project.

The alarm company's mark up on their payment plan is modified to their advantage giving the church what I perceive to be an unfair mark up on their equipment. If this is indicative to the project cost over runs, I am working hard at retrieving some of the church's money.

However, it remains to be difficult without having the proper paperwork. Right now, I am piecing together what I can find the best way I can. This is not how I want to approach the subcontractors and Phil. I am working on improving open communications daily and weekly in the Trustee Department. I have detailed the memos to remove a lot of ambiguity, presumptions and assumptions. This is one of the first steps to improving our Trustee Department's performance to be the best we can be.

I would like everyone to avail themselves to the fact; I will not be able to continue the pace at which I have been moving the project until we have satisfied the request for much needed information. Due to the already strong networking and setting up the track to run on for the Team Project Representatives, I would not like to have another false start when we get started again.

*Please refer to memo dated 7/18/2009 and subsequent memos for more clarifications.

Stay Bless,
Much Success"

THE CENTER

After numerous meetings and demand for church financial disclosure, Tessy gave me a cluster of file folders filled with an assortment of papers. The papers in the folders had no relevance to the project or the trustee board's signed agreement with me. By her withholding the Tabernacle's financial information, if she had left today or tomorrow, no one would really have a grip on what was going on with the church.

After mounting pressure and several meetings, mom gave permission to the trustee board members to check other trustees' desk for information that might be needed. I took advantage of this new policy; however, other board members felt apprehensive about looking for any information that was not given to them generously by Tessy. After looking through Tessy's desk, I found the bank covenant and loan agreements along with other important documents. The bank covenants had an agreement that read as such: if the church leadership regime decided, the Faith Educational and Community Center could be used for apartments or condominiums.

I found paperwork showing the Faith and Educational Center had a 501c3 status with the federal government. Initially Tessy was in favor of applying for federal grants. Once I retained a grant writer and the actual writing of the grants began, Tessy became resistive. She and the inner circle did not want to be held accountable to anyone about church funds. They then decided to take the option of applying for federal grants off the table. This left the entire financial burden for the center to be carried by the parishioners, which made it a heavy lift. I explained as best as I could that the center needed self-sustaining revenues in order to meet the vision of the pastor. My plea fell on deaf ears.

One of my initial tasks was to create a mission statement using a committee of volunteers I had recruited, calling them the Team Representatives. Subsequently, I was alarmed by an earlier mission statement I found that was never mentioned to me by Tessy or the inner circle. This mission statement's very clear purpose was to force the church's beliefs unto people, more so than a service to the community.

I also found the signed deed for the property, which was in Mother and Tessy's name. I was not comfortable with that, and I believed the parishioners were unaware of the possibility Tessy could take control and ownership of the Faith and Educational Community Center real estate.

God forbid if something were to happen to Mother or if the church satisfied the loan within the thirty-year fixed term. Tessy would have a free hand solely over this property. The Faith and Educational Center was not tax exempt, which required the Tabernacle Church to pay yearly real estate taxes. Being that the parishioners were actually paying for the Faith and Educational Center property from the Tabernacle Church treasury, I asked Tessy if the Faith and Educational Center was going to reimburse the Tabernacle Church. Tessy answered yes, but she had no paperwork or a plan on how this was going to be done. Keep in mind, the project at conclusion would cost the Tabernacle Church over 1.2 million dollars.

I referred to the Faith and Educational Center as Tessy's building and retirement estate bought and paid for by the Tabernacle Church membership. More alarming to me was the discovery of a second board used to secure the bank loan for the Faith and Educational Center. People on this new board were just as surprised as I to learn they were on a board they knew nothing about. This board for the Faith and Educational Center consisted of seven members. Of these, Tessy, Minister Lesley, and Reverend Helen were the only ones aware of this secret board while others contested that they did not know of its existence. Even though, signed documents indicated they were board members. Aside from all the secrecy and confusion, one of the members left the church over the Faith Educational Center's business affairs. Afterward, he became severely ill and passed away in 2009.

I noticed the bank held a lien on the Tabernacle Church in order to secure the building for the Faith and Educational Center. According to the loan agreement, if the church defaulted on the loan, the bank would make collection on both properties. Tessy was wielding and holding all of the church legal power in her hands. I observed how Mother would ramp up her congregants during sermons while addressing her dwindling audience by telling them, "We are doing the Faith and Education Center at 292 without one government dollar. This is what y'all are doing!" After this the parishioners stood to their feet applauding, with ear-piercing "Thank You, Jesus" as they danced into the aisles. At this point, I still was not sure if the church had money in the treasury or not.

I was not an authorized signatory, therefore unable to access any bank account information. Once I learned that there were at least three bank accounts being used, Tessy lost the signature cards I had signed. In light of these disclosures, I sent out yet another memo with alarms and bells to the organization. This memo is in its entirety giving a detailed view of the discord and dysfunction of the church leadership regime.

Re: Weekly Update of Affairs @Faith and Educational Community Center

Message:

Greetings Everybody,

Based on my own personal experience in getting needed paperwork I will counsel and recommend to my mother, Tessy, and both boards.

*Tessy, you might be too busy to sit on both boards, and it might not serve the Tabernacle, Inc., best of interest to have you on both boards. If things were getting done smoothly, I probably would have not noticed the apparent conflict of interest.

I recommend that no one person handle all the money and church business by themselves the way we are apparently doing it today. One person handling the entire business of the ministry is not an effective way to progress the ministry as I can attest to. Operating with one person handling the church money and other vital business can be detrimental to the ministry and its members. I see a great need to have more transparency among board members, being that we need to function as one body helping each other. I recommend you use a system to classify or declassify sensitive information.

There seems to be no rank and file, so we are working against the ministry. It appears that our real communications with what we should communicate is broken. E.g. I get no feedback or very little feedback about where the paperwork is after many weeks of requests.

I can only surmise that members are not able to have a two way dialogue with what should be the strongest department in the church. The Trustee Board controls the purse strings, and that is where the power of church business is. The Pastor should not have to worry about the money matters. We have to become her counsel to matters and allow the Pastor, than to make decisions. A decision maker makes decisions on the current information they have before them.

The Boards must become a wealth of accurate and current data to assist the Pastor in her decision making responsibilities. Our job is simply to supply the most up to date and current data we have. We are obligated to do that and deliver that information with accuracy, without omissions.

Last but not least, we have got to move into the 21st century, with updated communications and communicate more than we have in the past. If we are weak in our communication skills we will not be able to get the word out to our communities that Tabernacle church, Inc. is the place to be. We are now in business, so communication is a vital part of marketing what we do, and the survival to our visionary, and Pastor.

Aside from all the problems we are having every church member reserve the right to see certain church paperwork. Because we are incorporated we should be governed accordingly. Whether the paperwork is given voluntarily or with an injunction, membership has rights. Some of this behavior and secrecy is crossing over the line into Anti Trust Violations.

Hopefully these words will encourage us to be more attentive to do the right things. Stay blessed.

Through it all, I continued asking for bank statements, bank balances, and other stated documents. Part of the working plan for the center was to offer the community a hair salon. Before I left for my scheduled book tour in October, I hired three hair stylists. It was agreed that Tessy and Reverend Helen would manage the business of the hair salon during my absence. Instead, I get an e-mail from Mother telling me she had taken charge of the center and the hair salon in my absence. This move was orchestrated by Tessy, Mother, Reverend Helen, and the rest of the inner circle.

My plan was to continue with the business plan when I returned from my book tour in early November. When I arrived at the Faith Educational and Community Center, none of my keys worked. I was literally locked out of my mom's church and the Faith and Educational Center. I was told by a parishioner this lockout took place on October 18, 2009, when a locksmith changed the locks while they were attending the yearly anniversary appreciation service for my mother. I called my mother, asking incredulously, "Ma, why did you all lock me out of your church and the center?" She replied cynically, "I am the owner. I can do whatever I please. You locked yourself out." I said, "How is that? I don't understand. Why would I lock myself out?" The phone went quiet.

Breaking the silence I said, "Okay…I will talk with you later, have a blessed day." Ironically, the lockout came on the heels of my paperwork requests to Tessy before I left for my book tour. Not to bring further stress to my mom, I placed the entire project on indefinite hold until the leadership regime honored the contractual agreement. I reached out several times unsuccessfully by telephone to Tessy. She never returned my calls.

I elected to not pursue any further actions that would place Mother and parishioners into a legal predicament because of the behaviors of a church leadership regime gone rogue. Their maneuvers were nothing new. I had seen this tactic before. Often, the leadership regime would cower in the background behind Mother after their many destructive and malicious actions toward her family. I quietly dismissed myself, leaving the church regime to do what they thought best for the ministry and themselves. I notified the Team Project Representatives that we were in an indefinite holding pattern. They had been informed earlier of this possibility due to the inability to obtain paperwork.

In December, one of the hair stylists I had hired called me, saying, "Tessy and two others wearing crosses came into the salon for a meeting." They told us, "James is on his book tour and will be back soon." A second stylist got on the phone, saying, "They were lying to us for two months, saying you were coming back." The last stylist said, "I stayed until I couldn't take them any longer. They kept pressuring me to come to church. When I brought up problems at the shop, they ignored me." The stylist went on saying, "They kept saying you were going to return, so I tried to stay. You gave us direction and managed the place." I acknowledged the stylists with gratitude for hanging in there. I told them I had hoped the problems would have been resolved before it came to them leaving the salon.

At this point, Tessy was the most powerful person in the church. Tessy plotted and dug herself into a position to take full advantage of my mother and the congregants. She became extremely influential over my mother's decisions. Mom would act on Tessy's recommendations almost without contemplation.

My second time around allowed me to clearly see why she needed me out of the way. What was alarming to me is how she influenced decisions concerning who should be a member of the Tabernacle Church as well as who the department heads should be.

As I researched church deeds and the other church business that I could get access to, it was clear Tessy was running the corporate organization of the church singlehandedly. She needed and used my mother's preaching to collect the money. They held secrets about each other that forged a strong bond. While I sat at my desk on many occasions, they would stand with their backs to me whispering to each other.

Tessy created several falsehoods about her pastor's family, which kept my mother thinking that her children and grandchildren were against her. She assaulted our creditability with propaganda that held no merit. She cultivated and spun some yarn to my mom and others that were far from the truth, such as that I was an alleged drug dealer. By this point I had lost my inspiration and intent for any respectful reentry into the organization. The only thing left for me, my sister, and brother to do was to allow this church organization's regime to run its course. In January 2013, my brother sought to initiate better communication with mother with the intent to bring about a warmer family relationship. Despite his goodwill, mom disagreed with him on every topic, including his past unlawful eviction by sheriff deputies from the house. Through her responses, he gained more perspective on what mom had told her congregants and friends about this family matter. She told Steven he had picked her up and thrown her to the ground. Saddened, Steven said, "Mom, that never happened." In March 2013, mother admitted to Steven that she had impeded the progress of the center by telling Tessy not to cooperate with me. She feared I would uncover misappropriations of church funds for a second time.

One of the secrets Tessy held over mom's head was based on her own misguided counsel: Mom was not reporting any income to the Internal Revenue Service. This had gone on for years after my forced departure. Tessy and her certified public accountant, Dennis, had convinced my mother and tried to convince me her annual salary and offerings were gifts from the church and therefore nontaxable. I adamantly disagreed with Tessy and Dennis. So I went to the IRS Web site, found the tax code, printed and gave them a copy. I followed that up with this scripture: "Give to everyone what you owe them: If you owe taxes, pay taxes; if revenue, then revenue; if respect, then respect; if honor, then honor" (Romans 13:6–8 NIV).

Dennis was a heavy smoker. His reddening complexion had broken capillaries in and around his cheeks and he spoke with a raspy voice. At times his speech would break up as he'd breathe inward, followed with a deep, noisy, rattling, hacking cough and throat clearing as he gasped for air. At a second meeting, after Dennis had returned from one of his cigarette breaks, coughing vociferously, he told me again as if I did not understand, "Everything the pastor receives is a gift and is nontaxable." This time he added, "If the pastor reports all this money, it may raise attention from Uncle Sam."

Dennis was introduced as a certified public accountant. As I found out later he was Tessy's tax preparer, not a CPA. I thought it prudent for my mother to report her church income because of the amount of money she was collecting. In some years her cash salary was over three hundred thousand dollars. In the years immediately following Dad's death, I took over as head of household and carried mom as an exemption when the church was not capable of giving her a substantial salary. Once the financial climate of the church improved and she started receiving a substantial amount of money, I stopped carrying her as an exemption.

One day mom began to talk about her home going to be with the Lord. She detailed how her home-going service had to be over the top because of who she is. When she brought up this topic, I in turn raised my discontent over her lack of interest in purchasing a headstone for Dad and Grandma's grave sites. Upon my dad's death mom was the sole beneficiary to his insurance policies, entitlements, and state benefits. Mother became heated over this, ranting and saying she was going to spend every last dime on herself before she leaves this earth.

Over the years Tessy convinced my mother that she was the one looking after her interest and was her great protector. In the meanwhile it's Tessy who's running the church organization and pushing parishioners out of the church doors. She portrayed the other trustee board members as stupid and not to be trusted. Mom told me that a trustee named Mariah stole three thousand dollars during a church convention held in Newark, Delaware. I, like mom, had known Mariah for many years, and she was loyal to my mother. Bottom line, Mariah was not a thief. This was all Tessy's doing. It hurt Mariah when I questioned her about the money, and I apologized for even bringing it up. Turns out Tessy miscounted the money, and with my involvement it was resolved.

Tessy became more concerned about her influence as I began to counter her characterizations about the other board members. They were reluctant to challenge Tessy for fear of losing favor with their pastor. One trustee board member said to me, "Pastor believes everything Tessy tells her. Pastor can be rough." Another board member told me, "I get in trouble because I respect you and love you. What is wrong with that?" It had come to the point that board members were afraid to be seen talking with me. I never disclosed to anyone that mom was diagnosed with some dementia. People working closely with her noticed the confusion and fleeting thoughts. Tessy, Dosie, and a few recognized my mother's forgetfulness and took full advantage. A better term for Tessy and the inner circle is they *bewitched* our mother. Tessy wielded complete influence and control over mother's mind. I started to think, "Who is Tessy, and where did she come from?"

Without me or another family member being involved in the organization, Tessy had full control over the church's cash and finances. No pastor can keep up with the money in their church without the proper checks and balances. One of the outer circle ministers said to me, "I just pay my tithe and give my offerings. Sometimes my tithe is over two thousand dollars a month between my wife and me. What the pastor and the trustee board does after that I don't know. If they mishandled it, they will have to answer and give account to God on judgment day."

My response to the minister was, "I won't wait until judgment day arrives. If I suspect or see a problem, I will address it as a good steward. I would certainly pray about how to address the problem, however leaving the problem unsettled is not my nature.

This minister's viewpoint was typical of people who have no voice or say and are rendered powerless in their churches. When something is wrong, they find reasons as to why it is right. When something is factually correct, they argue as to why it's wrong. One inner circle minister used to say, "If prayer can't fix it, it can't be fixed." Preachers use this statement to sustain congregants in a state of helplessness, it keeps folks apathetic. So shut up and park yourself. We don't want to fix it, and it ain't going to change.

When I first arrived back on the scene the second time, I said to Mom and the inner circle, "Buying the building at 292 was a mistake. You got ripped off!" When I questioned how the trustees could let my mother walk into this situation, their answer was, "Pastor said God told her to buy the building." My response was only to shake my head in amazement. The more I challenged the leadership regime about their poor judgment and defective decision-making, the more I helped speed the way to my descent and demise for the second time around. Mom and her inner circle unleashed a campaign to pressure me into saying that God told her to buy the building. The leadership regime even initiated a rumor: "The only reason Deacon Alston came back to the Tabernacle was to see what he could get." I then decided to withdraw from the organization with my dignity intact.

Perhaps my skin was a little thicker the second time around, or maybe I was planned up and prayed up. I felt a major disappointment in my church leadership; however, my inner growth allowed me to have a forgiving heart toward Tessy and the leadership regime. After leaving the church organization, two of the outer circle ministers called me weekly, saying, "We need you, bro, desperately!" One minister openly admitted to me that "it is as if Tessy has taken over the pastor's mind." I continued to receive calls from different worshipers who were curious as to my whereabouts. I knew in my heart to go back would be a fool's errand. I explained as best as I could that my presence there would only serve to put undue stress on my mother. So the best solution was for me not to be there. This experience reinforced the lesson that you can only help those who want to help themselves. People will only be reasonable if they choose to be.

THE ADULT SON OF A PASTOR

LOOKING INTO MOM'S FAMILY HISTORY I discovered that well over one hundred years ago, incest had been a splotch to our family's legacy, by no fault of mom. Could this be the contributing root cause for the genetic misfiring of mom's personality, creating an open door for a rogue church leadership regime to step in and facilitate discord within our family? It wasn't until my brother, sister, and I were adults that Mom warned her parishioners to be careful who they bring into their homes around their small children. Mom said she made the mistake of being too trusting of preachers that were wolves dressed in sheep's clothing. In the early years, parishioners feared our mother because of her reputation of how hard she was on her children. Mom ruled her family with an iron fist, which we considered to be unfair and unbalanced. She held us to a higher standard well above any member in her organization. Mother's members adopted the saying, "If she can do that to her children, what will she do to me?" Mother was unrelenting in showing the world how hard she was.

I was in my fifties when the reality of my mother's actions could no longer be denied. Over the years, at different intervals, members who had left the ministry began to contact me to tell their stories of their

Tabernacle experiences. Members would tell me that I and my siblings were not in a position to see what was happening or what was being said about us, which was baffling to me. I had my first glimpse into understanding what people were talking about when my ex-wife Pauline divorced me.

During our marriage, Pauline was surrounded by one tragedy after another. The first tragedy had to do with her oldest child, Vanessa. Vanessa had plunged a steak knife into her boyfriend's chest, which he later died from at the Good Samaritan Hospital, in Suffern, New York. Her daughter said she was afraid of her boyfriend, who was abusive to her. I thought we were good people, and this kind of stuff does not happen to churchgoing believers. The judge set bail at $50,000. Pauline pleaded with me to pay the bail so Vanessa could go home to her two small children. Her daughter was eventually acquitted on self-defense.

The next sad tragedy dealt with Bobby, her son. Bobby got caught up with the wrong crowd. He was stabbed multiple times with an ice pick in the streets of the village of Spring Valley, New York. The police detectives said his death was the result of a drug deal gone bad in an area of the village known for drug dealing called the Hill. This left me spinning in unfamiliar territory, learning quickly about a subculture outside of my life experience. While these tragedies were foreign to me, I supported her through them.

A lot of folks thought I divorced Pauline when in fact she divorced me, suing me for nearly two years. It was when I found photos of Pauline in another man's arms that our real tribulations began. While reviewing our credit reports before purchasing the house in Stony Point in 1999, I discovered an active loan for a Toyota Camry. I asked Pauline about the car. She claimed she didn't know anything about it. After confronting her several times with the photos, she wrote me a letter asking me for a divorce. She stated she wanted to move on with her life. I gratefully honored her request to dissolve the marriage. During the court proceeding, depositions, and discovery process, it came to light that Pauline was paying for her boyfriend's car. She tried desperately through her attorney to obtain the house I bought with mom. Pauline came to the marriage with no wealth or property yet wanted my stocks, bonds, pension, and 401k. Ms. Gargotta, Pauline's lawyer, her boyfriend, and

Pauline wanted what they called the big house included in the divorce settlement.

During the divorce preceding, my mother stood determinedly with Pauline. She went so far as to sit next to Pauline during the court proceeding across the aisle from me. How bizarre is that? Mom said, "The Bible says to stand with the accused." This statement left me bewildered.

I spent a great deal of time and energy protecting my mother who lived in that same house my ex-wife so desperately tried unsuccessfully to include in her divorce settlement.

When Pauline ran out of money, my mother told her to keep going and that she would help her with pursuing the case against me. As her civil suit continued, I pleaded with Pauline to stop trying to take the house my mother lives in. At one point she stated strongly, "I only have one mother and her name is Dorothy, and I don't give a damn about your momma." When I told mom what Pauline said, her response was, "You can't get her to say it to my face." After all the support my mother gave Pauline, she lost her case against me and left the Tabernacle Church. Our union was dissolved in 2002 after almost fourteen years of marriage.

Growing up in our house we never spent the holidays with just family members. Mother insisted on having a church visitor. That person seemed to be there to observe our family, or at least the pastor's kids. As I aged, I could see a major disconnect between mom and the family. I, my brother and sister were in constant competition with mom's congregation. Over the years, through business relationships people seemed to be surprised that I was not the person they heard I was. This discord between the church and the family was manufactured by our mother. She painted herself and her family into an illusion to her congregants, leaving no room for making things right other than wishing poor will unto the pastor's family. Left unchallenged, illusions become realities. Through subtleties and direct comments, Mom used her psychology and bully pulpit to lead her congregants and friends into believing her children were villainous to her. Her stories were carefully thought out and crafted to negatively manipulate parishioners' thoughts and behaviors toward their family. The parishioners over the years faced negative sound bites coming over the pulpit about their pastor's children.

Some parishioners felt a need to contact me out of confusion. Deep down inside they knew what they were hearing was not true. I could tell in their voices they felt powerless, caught under the spell of not knowing what to do. Afraid to speak out about family values, it was just easier to stay under the radar and go with the flow. Besides, parishioners were taught and trained they could not survive in any other church. Parishioners saw the Tabernacle Church and my mother as their only ticket to heaven.

The reason mom positioned herself as being victimized by her children was to gin up and garner sympathy from her congregations and fellow ministers. I use the word *congregations* because the church became a revolving door as many members came and left. I calculated that if the Tabernacle Church was able to sustain its followers through a progressive leadership, the church would have had well over two thousand members belonging to the organization.

As we matured, we became more aware of mom's over-bearing and unreasonable behavior. It became unacceptable to us. When it got out of hand, mom's only solution to repair what she had done was to occupy her time pitting the church against her children. As children, we tried to do the right thing by letting mom have her way. After a while, the family could no longer bear the abuse and continue going off into the night quietly. Rather than ending the abuse, the church leadership regime took sides with mother to punish and discredit us openly and behind closed doors. There was no way out of our dilemma other than mom mitigating the misuse of her family and owning up to her misstep. As a diversion, mom and the inner circle kept the minds of the people focused on her persecution or some type of problematical demons attacking her. In return the inner circle would bamboozle a few people to chasing after these allusions while plainly mowing down anyone in their way. I feel in my heart that mom is beloved by those who felt a calling to serve in protecting the pastor from these mystical spirits and demons. I and others have experienced the seriousness of those functioning in this capacity. Mother would often say to her congregants, "You can't see these spirits with your natural eye. These spirits are demonic that come after me, the godhead," as she often referred to herself. Words can be very powerful. The Bible says that if you are a Christian, you have power over all demons.

Once I stepped back, I was able to see the topography of Tabernacle Church. Mother and the inner circle would cascade rumors to the congregation that created mistrust among the churches they visited. I remember an occasion when Mother came home from a church service in Middletown, New York. She called for a pressing meeting with her inner circle to tell the story of how Deacon Danny literally put his butt in her face in the church dining room when the deacon bent over as he was picking something up from the floor. Mom said he was being disrespectful and was telling her "to kiss his butt." She played the role of the anointed vexed woman of God. I watched the group shaking their heads from side to side, some saying, "Umh...umh...umh..." Others were saying softly, "Oh my God..." Some put their heads down, moving their lips as if they were in silent prayer and in communication with God. Mom and the rogue leadership regime worked tenaciously, beating their drum of propaganda that we were mean-spirited children. My sister's car mechanic asked her if it was true that mom's grandson hit her in the church. The rumor was spreading like wildfire, and upon hearing it, the grandchildren were adversely affected by distress and pain. My sister and I called mom about the rumor. She used word games, saying in an increasingly annoyed voice, "I didn't say he hit me. I said *if* he had hit me." There is an old adage: if you say it long enough, people begin to believe what you are saying. However, there is another saying: truth travels slowly, and a lie will outrun the truth every time.

One such rumor caught the attention of my friend of over forty years who has a twenty-five-year-plus career in law enforcement. Mom and the Tabernacle leadership alleged that I was a drug addict and drug dealer. My ex-wife had told people I was smoking crack while lying on the family room floor and she couldn't get me up. This was happening as I, my mother, and ex-wife lived in the same house and attended the same church. My friend laughed when he heard the story in his county, thinking it to be hilarious and at the same time preposterous.

My then wife continued to feed mom with narcissistic, irrational, unfounded allegations, which only served to enhance her dismal delusions. It was easier for folks, including my ex-wife, to give in to my mother's whimsical flings of untruths and behavior than to pay the price of disagreeing with her. The inner circle emboldened mom's schemes to a misguided congregation. It wasn't just her family that was affected, but many left Tabernacle due to the anger, shame, and hurt brought on by the inner circle gang. They, along with Tessy, were responsible for spinning our mother into a toxic state of ignorance. The inner circle led mother to believe her decisions were of God and that she and God were melded into one. Tessy and the inner circle had mom believing she was incapable of making a mistake. In private, often she would say "No one can find a spot or blemish in my life." The inner circle convinced her that pastors in the county respected and feared her when she walked into their churches.

The real big gun was Minister Lesley. Les would canvass other churches to search out unhappy congregation members. When he found someone who appeared discontented, he would befriend them by chumming around with them. Over time, his gift of smooth talking would persuade them out of their present church and into the Tabernacle Church's membership. To this day I remember Lesley approaching Mom saying he was close to hooking another church's member: "I think she is going to join the church. We almost have her. I told her she belongs at the Tabernacle Church, not in that dead church she's at now."

Eventually, the inner circle began feeding on themselves, a true feeding frenzy. Unbeknownst to mom they were fighting like cats and dogs—backstabbing each other. For me it was sobering to see the level of ruthlessness as cross-wearing Christians went at each other. The inner circle knew they had to grace mom with the best piece of gossip they could find or manufacture.

They especially enjoyed making fun of the churches they fellowshipped with. One in Spring Valley, New York, they called Buckingham Palace. And if that was not enough, they said the church smelled, literally. Well, that church lost a few key members to Tabernacle.

The inner circle fed into Mom's narcissism by telling her that Tabernacle was the best and most perfect church around. They continued planting the seed of why the church membership had dwindled from five hundred members to about forty: there was too much God in the Tabernacle Church for people. The leadership regime held such contempt and religious elitisms toward other churches until it became outlandish.

I commend those church parishioners who were innocent bystanders for being there for our mother in a good way. It was the inner circle that sustained Mom's riding of the one-trick sympathy pony for years. They fed into her complaining that the family was not physically supporting her by attending honoree celebrations. The way I describe the situation between the family and the inner circle: Someone telling you to open the door and come in yet they haven't released the deadbolt. For those that have and still take clear advantage by fueling mom's mind and behavior with vain worship, I can only say shame on them.

Mom's choice not to have any of her children involved with her ministry and to not implement sound systems of accountability created a runway for financial misappropriations. With her need for unbridled attention, the inner circle's *bewitching*, and an ill-advised congregation, the opportunity for the perfect storm was created in the Tabernacle Church.

Over the years I developed a friendly relationship with Associate Pastor Caudell (major) of a church under the Tabernacle's Church ministry located in Atlanta, Georgia. He and his wife were the co-pastors and had no problem getting onto mom's favorite list. They knew just how to cater to her unyielding need for attention. When mom would arrive at the Hartsfield-Jackson Airport, Caudell would have a full motorcade with a motorcycle escort whiz mom from the airport. Mom was flattered by it all. I asked mom who pays for all of that. She replied, "I don't know, Major takes care of all that, I am a servant of God. God gives me favor." His wife would come to New York each year for mom's annual anniversary, the holy convocation, and her three-day birthday services.

On one particular trip mom set me up with Caudell's wife to talk with me. I was to drive the pastor to the Palisades Mall, drop her off, and mom was to pick her up later. Once Pastor started asking me questions, and by her body language and tone, unsuspecting me realized Pastor was convinced mom's three children were villains and against their mother. I remember the gist of her conversation was, "If there are three of you, why can't there be four?" We seemed to not be able to get past this question when my reply was, "What do you mean?" I was not catching on to what she was talking about, and she only continued to take me in a circle with her conversation. We sat at the mall curbside for quite some time as she continued with this charade. Finally, I asked the pastor, "Would you allow your church people to talk against your kids and attack your son or daughter?" The pastor answered in a contemptuously softer tone, her head slightly downward, "No, I wouldn't, not my children."

Some years later I learned from mom that Pastor Caudell, who was second in command of the Fulton County Sherriff Department, was undergoing a federal investigation. Fulton County, Georgia, was under investigation for accounting irregularities on Pastor Caudell's watch. The county was looking for several million dollars unaccounted for. When I heard the news, I spoke with Caudell. He told me that if he was indicted, he would no longer be able to afford to pay the mortgage on their home. Caudell was eventually convicted and sentenced to federal prison in El Paso, Texas. This is where he mysteriously died on a Sunday morning in his jail cell, serving less than half of his sentence. The money was recovered, all accept for $500,000. Pastor Caudell was directly connected to the misplaced money. Caudell's misstep and death caught the eye of national news. This was another grave casualty of one of our pastors behind the cross.

Those close to mom enabled her to regard her family as throwaway people, through their vain worship of her. The harsh reality is our mother started a devout family among her church congregation rather than nurturing her begotten family. We, her children, became strangers while the Tabernacle Church replaced us. In allowing congregants to believe she had no family support system, mother garnered sympathy. Often given the victim's chair by the inner circle, she now became victimized by those same hands. For over forty-five years, mom gained a ferocious appetite for compliments and ego stoking.

As the congregation shrank, the inner circle placed added burdens on the congregants by increasing their assessments each year for mom's anniversary. In some cases parishioners would call me for assistance or to express tearfully how they did not have the money. Several times I laid out a proposal to include a church anniversary along with the pastoral anniversary. The inner circle vetoed my proposal, saying it would detract from the pastor's celebration. Instead, Tessy and the inner circle sought to appease mom by having revivals on her birthday in February. They bent over backward to showcase to the world mom adulating herself in the performance of God's duties.

The inner circle fell into a pattern of hyping and showboating m's success. One year I sent a telegram to be read in church the morning of mom's anniversary service. Tessy and the inner circle made a big deal out of my absence and convinced mom not to read it to the congregation. Later I asked for the telegram back. One of the deacons took pains to let me know he retrieved the wrinkled telegram from my mother's office trash can. That telegram cost me $128 to send. I ask Mom why it wasn't read at the service. Mom's reply was, "You should have saved your money." Our family could no longer compete with the volume of gifts and vain worship bequeathed on mom. I recognized that she felt loved when she was receiving gifts and services from others. This was clearly her love language.

I believe if the inner circle loved my mother, they would have not conspired against her family, competing against her children. A reliable source informed me they were leading the congregation into chanting and wishing ill will upon Mom's family. A parishioner called to say the in-the-dark parishioners were saying, "God is going to get them children." At my grandmother's home-going service eulogy, Minister Lesley took the microphone and said, "God took the pastor's mother to lighten the pastor's load and burden so she could continue to go forth in the ministry."

I sat quietly in the front row of the church next to mom thinking, *I know he didn't say that.* I couldn't help but wonder if Les really meant or even believed what he said. Or was he playing to mom and the crowd? It took me a few moments to gather my senses. My interpretation of what Les said was God killed our grandmother, the pastor's mother, in order to get her out of the way of the ministry. When things settled down, I asked my family if I had heard Les correctly. They all said I did. Even mom agreed. However, mom would not say that Minister Les's statement was inappropriate.

SURVIVAL INSTINCTS OF
A PASTOR'S FAMILY

OUR GRANDMOTHER Ms. ANNIE C. Thomas, "mother Thomas," expired in the Northern Manor Nursing Home in Nanuet, New York. When dementia rendered our grandmother incapable of caring for herself, mom decided to place her into Northern Manor.

Mom did share with me a story, possibly one of the last remembrances of Grandma. She said she went to visit Grandma, and during the visit she leaned forward to say good-bye. According to mom, Grandma slapped the daylights out of her. I laughed and said you are the daughter and, she is still the mother. This story brought back memories of how Grandma used to cry often. She would tell me that mom hurt her feelings by dressing her down in front of people. The pastor's children and grandchildren have never been motivated by poor intent or ill will toward anyone. There was no reason for the contempt or the mean-spiritedness. Whenever I questioned the inner circle, they would just go silent as I assured them I wouldn't treat their mother in this manner.

Their reaction only furthered their actions. By reporting to my mother, they were being attacked by me.

The most disheartening for my family is how the inner circle continues to stomp on our family while protecting their own, except for Minister Les. Minister Les followed my mother's lead, throwing his family and grandchildren to the wind. The church's inner circle allowed their pastor to believe that her every thought and utterance—be it right, wrong, agreeable, or disagreeable—is always absolutely God driven. They themselves condoned her unnatural behavior in their *bewitching*, instead of countering it with "They are your children. We, the church, love them as your children."

We were treated as if we were Satanic, out to diminish our own mother's ministry. My mother went as far as to blame me for her illnesses at a time when I was not even near her. After I approached her about it, she later rescinded her statement and changed her position in an e-mail to me. However, I am sure she did not make that change to her inner circle or congregation.

Driven by their own passionate zeal to keep mom isolated from her family, the inner circle became the obstructionist to mom's well-being and physical health. In 2000, early one morning, mom became ill in the master bedroom with an elevated blood pressure of 212. I was down the hall asleep approximately twenty-five feet away. Mom says she became disorientated and could only think to call Minister Lesley on his cell phone.

Minister Lesley called my sister, whom he is not fond of. He paraded around, wasting valuable time avoiding and evading my sister's question as to why he needed my cell number. He refused to inform my sister that Mom had contacted him and was not feeling well. By this time mom was standing at my door calling my name, saying "I'm sick, I'm sick," while leaning on the door frame. I jumped up caught her before she fell to the ground. I directed mom to hold on to me while I slowly walked her back to her bed. I took her blood pressure. It was 212. I don't remember what the bottom number was. Mom was insisting she was not going to the hospital. I dread the thought if I were not there, if Dosie or one of the others in the inner circle would have allowed her to lie there with the danger of being in a stroke zone.

I called my sister with the blood pressure reading. My sister responded with, "You have to get her out of there now. You have to get her out of there. That's too high." Mom was saying all the while I made the two calls that she was not going to the hospital. I called 911, and mom was transported to Good Samaritan Hospital in Suffern, New York. Mom's blood pressure continued to elevate on the way to the hospital. After this, mom was safely cared for. Once again, I ask the inner circle folks to please call me or one of mom's family members in case of any emergency health issues with our mother. In July 2011 mom was taken to the emergency room by Reverend Helen. Minister Lesley works at the hospital knowing our mother was there. Neither one called me or a family member.

When I approached Reverend Helen about this, she was acceptable of the conversation and committed that it would not happen again. I called Minister Lesley who began to argue with me. He was arguing over notifying me or a family member regarding any urgent situation with our mother. After arguing and dancing me around on the phone for ten minutes, he said crossly, "Okay!" I said to Lesley. "Did Mom tell you not to call me?" He says, "Mom has never told me not to call you." I thought, *Then why in God sake wouldn't you call me?* I ended this charade by saying, "If it were your mother, I would not do that to you." I politely said "Have a good day" and closed my cell phone. I spent the next two months taking mom for a battery of tests. Thanks be to God all her tests were negative.

Tessy and the inner circle were above reproach in mom's eyes. Mother often placed Tessy into a false light by offering up accolades to Tessy before the congregants. Mom would do this ritual sometimes just before her sermons. Mom would say to the congregants on occasions, "Poor Tessy drags herself out to the house of God and the Faith and Educational Center up at 292 with her swollen ankles to check on the electricians every day." She would say to the congregants, "Amen y'all." The congregants instantly responded thunderously in harmony, "Amen."

Mom had this knack for misrepresenting the facts about Tessy and the inner circle folk. They had the okay to do and say whatever they pleased to whomever they wanted. Most of the congregants would tell me about the disdain they held for Tessy and some of the others. I learned over the years that mom took on an unmovable position in her view of people. You were either right or wrong. It was never about agreement or disagreement. It was God or Satan, period. I recall one of her inner circle members who worked in a bank coming to the trustee office saying, "Praise the Lord, everyone." As he leaned against the door frame looking toward board member Sister Green, he announced, "Sister Green, I was looking at your accounts. You have a lot of money in the bank." Sister Green sat with her mouth open in disbelief while looking perplexed. Mom would defend these things to me by saying, "Don't accuse Tessy, Lesley, Dosie, and others of wrongdoings. That would be a direct reflection on me." Mom continued by saying, "They didn't do anything wrong." Maybe mom is right. My family instinct tells me different. If they are not true believers, then they have nothing to worry about today.

A smart, genuine Christian is able to stand in the gap without being disrespectful, with no regard to person. A professing genuine Christian is one who is able to man up to poor and unacceptable behavior in themselves and others. A weak-kneed Christian is full of finger-pointing and, excuses refusing to see the error of their behaviors. I see the thread of cronyism running throughout my mother's church organization. The inner circle is focused on self-serving purposes, self-gain, and loyalty to themselves.

Mother could not free herself from being a pastor and prophet when it came to fundamental conversations with her family or in her parent-child relationships. I noticed in the late 1990s how mom became a pseudo listener during family conversations that were not to her liking. Her divisiveness made reasoning with her unattainable. If mom did not like what she was hearing, she would straight away switch the conversation saying, "I am the mother" or "I am the pastor." She would go back and forth between these two positions instead of just being our mom. The conversations would then spiral into confusion, no matter the subject. She would warn us, "Don't bring up anything about the Bible because I will run circles around you. That's why I always win!"

We are her begotten children, not her parishioners. Having a relatively normal conversation became virtually impossible under any circumstances as Mom would become combative with her children and her grands.

The latest round of allegations by Tessy and the inner circle was over the top. While driving mom to one of her doctor's appointment, Mom says, "You always put me down." She followed up with, "You all hate me. A lot of people hate me. I know it." After Mom finished speaking, she went into a long maniacal laugh, leaving me speechless. Rather than debate the issue, I asked her why she felt that way and could she give me some specific examples. She said she could not think of any. I knew then Tessy was behind this allegation once again. This allegation has gone on for more than two decades with no clear facts or examples of what she is talking about. I said finally out of frustration, "Who is telling you this?" Well, that triggered her to stand up on her hind legs. Mom turned her head to the left, elevating her voice one level below a yell, saying, "There you go again, accusing me of having no mind of my own!" I said, "Come on, Mom, you are going a bit far. This discussion is based on inaccurate or no facts, unfounded accusations."

Mom continues to push the envelope as far as she can to prove to a few interested folks she is being neglected by her children. Her mission to hide and keep her skeletons in the closet has no limitations, no boundaries, or spending caps. As I suggested earlier, skeletons don't like closets. I have come to accept the reality of *it is what it is.* The inner circle was extremely successful, convincing mom that her family was her rival. Any problems or deficiencies that arose in the church, the inner circle found a way to point to her children. When we had worked in her ministry, we took the blame for any little thing that went awry. When we weren't in the church, we took the hit for things not being right because we should have been there to make it right—it was a losing proposition. The church leadership time and again put on view a double standard to almost everything. It's a basic principle. You can't subvert and support situations at the same time. The leadership regime created mass confusion among its congregants. The analogy I use to describe our family's situation with the inner circle would be that if I were to walk out into water during a storm to save a small child from drowning, the Tabernacle leadership regime would say to mom and its congregants, "James can't swim." Some of us lived across the country and in different states; however, they found a way to point fingers in our direction for their own dysfunction and ineptness.

More importantly, She was supposed to be a mother first and a pastor second. Our sacrifice has been greater than anyone could ever imagine or begin to understand. We lost our mom over what should not have been. This is supposed to be *church*, not some cold profit-focused corporate organization. I found myself working with a spirit of darkness and sophisticated ignorance. Showing family presence at church events is not good enough. What makes a family is a spiritual bond. It is the sight unseen, not some outward appearance to fool a few people. The family was no longer willing to be placed on display, propped at a dais table by the inner circle to be made fools of for their frolic.

Dosie slithered her way into Mom's personal life by befriending her with vain worship and praise, along with unprecedented attention. Dosie was consumed by her obsession to be mom's daughter. She publicly declares how she would do anything to be inclusive, just anything to be part of the family. Dosie's fixation drove her to several attempts to corral Steven into marriage. According to Steven, the matrimony took place while they were in California. Steven said he had the marriage annulled. However, Dosie doesn't give the impression she is detached from Steven.

Let me give a little bit of background on the youngest of mom's children, the one I used to call my baby brother. Steven attended Taft College in California, a two-year school on a full track–and-field scholarship. He holds records for his high school athletic ability in Rockland County, New York. He earned his BA from California State University at Bakersfield where he was awarded a second full scholarship in track and field. He then served in the US Navy as an electronics warfare technician and ship's broadcast journalist. His rank was third-class petty officer. Assigned to the missile cruiser USS *Jouett*, Steven served his country in Desert Shield and Desert Storm under President George H. W. Bush. Later he earned his master's degree from Regent University. Dosie's marriage quest pushed her to the limits. She traveled the world in her vain efforts to be at every port that Steven was scheduled to arrive in order to win my brother over. She would send herself roses at work, pretending they came from my brother, while he was stationed in Korea and other countries around the world. Eventually, Dosie's coworkers caught on to what she was doing, and she became the laughingstock of her workplace.

The late bishop Charles Reid from New York City and a member of Pilgrim Assemblies Inc. was a frequent visitor in mom's church. He would frequently pull me to the side telling me that I was to be the next pastor of mom's church. While the bishop was ministering to the congregation, he called Dosie to the front of the church. She stood there with an ACE bandage around her right ankle, which seemed to have become part of her habitual dress code. As he began to pray for her, he asked, "Do you have a mother?" Dosie responded softly, "Yes."

The bishop made a heartfelt response to her and the congregation, saying clearly, "All the while I have been coming to this church observing how you serve your pastor, by all indications I thought you had no mother." He continued, "That is your mother sitting right here in the front row?" Again Dosie says, "Yes." The bishop said, "Well…well…" He looked at Dosie's mother and out over the congregation as if you could have pushed him over with a feather. Turning to Dosie, he said, "God is leading me to say to you, 'Spend more time with your mother.'" After the bishop's prophecy, Dosie's uncle, her mother's eldest brother, passed away unexpectedly. On the day of the funeral, I asked Dosie if she was going to attend. She gave me a depressing "yeah," but she never left the house. Instead, she sat in our family room with mom watching television rather than going to her uncle's memorial. Dosie appeared to abandon her mother and family in their time of bereavement.

As so many have before, Dosie played to Mom's flawed family values and weakened family principles. She doubled down on her insincere efforts by isolating mom from the family. Dosie knew how to work Mom, bestowing accolades on her while taking any abuse Mom dished out. Whenever Mom and Dosie argued, Mom would claim she fired Dosie. Dosie would soon slither back on her knees, begging Mom to give her another chance. Mom seemed to get some type of fulfillment from this show of loyalty. Through Dosie's tricks and street savvy, she learned how to cozy up to mom to the extent Mom made her the executrix of her will. Dosie was able to influence and scam Mom to share all her financial information with her. She gained access to mom's safety deposit boxes that contained cash, usually in amounts in excess of one hundred thousand dollars. When my younger brother was in good standing with her, mom placed his name on these bank boxes.

As the children, we refused to be the recipients of abuse from the inner circle and mom. Under the influence of Tessy and the inner circle, mom detached her personal business and finances from her family. She placed her business matters into the hands of Tessy, Reverend Helen, and Dosie. If Dosie sensed any glimmer of a relationship developing with mom and her children or grands, she would become silently hostile, obstructive, and divisive. She went so far as to form an alliance with one of mom's adjutants to initiate a rumor, telling unsuspecting congregants I had fathered a child out of wedlock and the child was four weeks old. Dosie instigated this rumor as mom was being thrust into the spotlight over Minister Leslie and Serika's marriage that was supposedly made in heaven.

In 2004, Dosie and mother filed a police report against me with the Stony Point Police Department, which was deemed falsified by the investigating detective. The report said I was the prime suspect in stealing and cashing in $12,000 worth of saving bonds. The bonds were payable to my three nephews. When they were born, mom asked me what she could do toward helping them with their college education in the future. I suggested she purchase saving bonds for them. I remember seeing the bonds, and at maturity they would have amounted to approximately twelve thousand dollars.

Dosie and my mother set up this grand plot thinking my arrest would be imminent. I was never so shocked, infuriated, or embarrassed by their intent and behavior. Long story short, at the end of the day the detective said, "Mr. Alston, your mother put you down as a prime suspect. I kept going by the house every week, and her story kept changing. She was not being honest with me." I kept the police report where the detective wrote across the face of the report, "Unsubstantiated." The detective went on to say, "Mr. Alston, don't worry about the allegations by your mother. There won't be any record of this complaint against you." I left the police station and drove directly to the house, infuriated by Dosie and Mom's actions. Short of initiating charges against Dosie for filing a false police report, I confronted her and Mom in the kitchen with the report in my hand. Mom's response was, "I told you about the saving bonds. You told me to call the police. Dosie didn't do anything wrong." All I could do was look at them standing there side by side, shaking my head in defeat and frustration. Through all my disappointment, I could only think of this passage: "Do not accuse anyone for no reason when they have done you no harm" (Proverbs 3:30 NIV).

My brother Steven was in the house at the time when mom accused me of stealing the saving bonds. Here is my brother's account of what he saw and understood about the accusations: "When Mom had misplaced the savings bonds, I witnessed and listened to her rant on and on about blaming you for stealing the savings bonds set aside for her grands and your nephews. She accused you of being a thief and needing to call the police to have you arrested.

"She was so driven about having you jailed. It almost seemed that nothing would satisfy her more than you behind bars. I watched all of this and couldn't understand why she wanted that for you as her son. I told her at the time that 'I don't believe James did this,' but she was too driven on her path of destruction. That's when I began to realize how wrong and crazy this all was, and she had become poison to all of us, and my eyes were just beginning to open to that truth. Her plan was to destroy your reputation and create limitations in your life by associating you with criminal behavior. This would have had terrible repercussions and place limitations upon you regarding certain future aspirations."

Sadly and to my confusion, when I retrieved the police report from the Stony Point Police, my brother Steven was listed as one of three complainants with Mom and Dosie. Steve never contemplated I would ever see the police report to this day. Mom had given money to some of the inner circle's children. A few of the parents quietly shared information with others about the large sums of money they had received. Some members were brazen enough to brag about the thousands of dollars Pastor had put into their hands. To this day, my nephews have never seen the saving bonds or money their grandmother told me she had put away for them. As was often the case, Mom and her inner circle worked backward to create stories that would best fit and support their agendas. I began to understand why the inner circle could not be upstanding. Their pastor was bankrolling them. They were bought and paid for.

I thought about the sound bites that Mom had created over the years. How she would say expressively in the pulpit and over the phone to her friends, "All I ever wanted since I was a little girl is my family."

In the final stages of my divorce proceeding, Pauline blamed mom for the discord in our marriage. Though, she disclosed to me that mom had encouraged her and financially supported her to go after me with the civil suit, I do remember Pauline had asked if we could move several times. What she was saying and I wasn't hearing was that she needed to get away from my mother. After all was said and done, Pauline attempted to apologize in the best way she knew how.

Mom went down to her church clothed in drama, whispering propaganda and leaking falsehoods that I stole $12,000 from her. Some people actually continue to think that I did this. Even now, mom still has not bothered to go back to her congregants and friends to legitimize the truth about her begotten family. She has never seized the opportunity to turn a wrong into right, or upright the ship. Mom, Dosie, and the church leadership left the congregants with misguided allegations and bogus information about the saving bonds and countless other stories. On another occasion, one of the ushers, alarmed and sickened by what she heard from the pulpit, called me.

She was upset and confused because the pastor was saying, "One of my children is sending me harassing e-mails" and that she was going to the police over it. I assured the person it was untrue. I immediately called my brother and sister to say Mom was really losing it. All we could do at this point was laugh in order to not cry. Being a pastor's child is a tough calling, filled sometimes with dark moments and embarrassing situations. No matter how good things appear, being a pastor's child is not a bed of roses. I pray relentlessly for pastors' children.

Even though their circumstances may be different from our own, the relativity is the same. If you are a pastor's child, you are open to harsh church and public scrutiny.

I am reminded of a dismal truth about a thief at the Tabernacle Church. Ironically, while twisted, this occurrence has audacity and merit. The woman was a member of the Tabernacle for over twenty years. She worked at Nyack Hospital in the billing and accounting department. Mom's head trustee at the time became severely ill, requiring hospitalization with what he said was a blood disorder. He had no health insurance and the hospital stay ended up costing many thousands of dollars. The church member did him the favor of removing his $60,000 hospital stay from the billing system. Earlier, this lady publicly informed mom, her inner circle, and the congregants of having repeated dreams of my brother Steven stealing from our mother. Short of being prosecuted she was fired from her tenured position at the hospital. She left the church out of embarrassment.

Sure, lots of folks leave churches due to corruption. I believe most have departed churches with a broken heart and lost hope in their church's leadership. A church should be in a position to truly help and serve people, not continually run entertainment centers, taking people's money and abusing them. I ask where my church was when their pastor needed accurate information and godly support. I ask where the church leadership support was when their pastor's children needed spiritual direction. We had no one reach out to us to say "I don't know what to do, but I am praying for you and your family.' Just those words would have brought sunshine to a cloudy day. I have come to the realization many churches are not equipped to handle severe problems or families in crisis. My brother, sister, and I reached out to several bishops and ministers. They were the ones we thought could help us. There appears to be an unwritten code with tribal secrecy among some leadership regimes, at least in the circles mom traveled in. This unspoken code, called "Protecting the body of Christ," appears to diabolically underscore what they say they're doing. Basically, if there was something not biblically ethical, it was convenient to overlook the matter, saying the Bible said we should protect the body of Christ. The unwritten code seemingly adjusted itself to money and faces. The only times I did not see the code enacted was when pastors had personal conflicts with each other. What I saw then were church congregations turning competitively hostile toward the other to the point of fisticuffs.

As a family searching for aid and solutions, we sat down with the late pastor, Bishop Sidney Buxton. He said to us, "Yeah, your mother was a missionary in my church. When I disagreed with her over what was God and what was not of God, your mother got up and left, telling me she was going to get a church out of a church." The bishop said, "It sounds as if your mother has some form of a character flaw." He went on to recommend we do two things to remediate our dilemma—first, to buy a three-dollar Hallmark card with these words imprinted or written,

"Please forgive us, we apologize" and second, "give the card to her and everything would be all right." At the end of our talk, the bishop prayed with us and gladly accepted the one hundred dollar bill I pulled from my pocket and handed him.

The bishop jarred me when he said, "Apologize." For a moment my thoughts went back to Minister Lesley. I recalled years back when Minister Les had given me a halfhearted apology. I couldn't remember why he apologized; however, seared into my mind was how he went about it. Les's words were "Forgive me for what you said I did to you" as he turned and walked away. Weeks later, we talked with the late Pastor Taylor, who had left the Tabernacle Church over some type of discord with Mom and the leadership regime well over thirty-five years ago. He did not pastor a megachurch; however, we found comfort through his encouragement. He prayed for our family then, and I believe daily. He never exploited our dignity with gossip. He called often to follow up, checking to see how we were doing. Pastor Taylor, I will never forget the respect, care, kind words, and encouragement you provided to us. You never put your hand out for anything in return for talking with us, praying with us, and being a friend.

After all the verbal profundity and looking through a spiritual prism, most churches appear incapable of treating nothing more than non-life-threatening superficial wounds. Some churches have failed in not reaching the core of real people's issues and problems. They offer no help for the severe situations that emerge within their congregations. Yes, they can visit the sick, eulogize a funeral, open the church for a wedding, and even tell you they will pray with or for you. "Don't worry everything is going to be all right." These are all reinforced warm, fuzzy things and words. But where is the real help from the Christians, the saved, the sanctified folk, Holy ghost filled, tongue talkers, and the prophets that walk among us?

With all the sermons, the shouting, the dancing, speaking in tongues, the moaning, rolling around on the ground, churches remain paralyzed to act on the Word of God they sing and preach about. It bothered me that churches can fall into a helpless state of nonspiritual, do-nothing state of mind. If this has happened to me being the son of a prominent pastor, what are others feeling and going through?

If you visit mom's church today, you will see a beautiful edifice, not the sacrifice, spiritual and financial support the family has given. Mom has money in the bank, cash stashed away. She has the house, not a happy home. She drives the finest of automobiles and has the parishioners and Dosie fussing over what she should wear. However, at the end of the day, who is really served? What is the worth for real peace of mind in Christ? mom said to me in later years, "When you all left from my church, it seemed as if all the brain power left."

A PASTOR'S FAMILY IN CRISIS

I CAME OUT OF SILENCE to write this book because of the love I have for our mother and my endearment to the congregants. Silence doesn't spare the people we love. Sometimes it hurts them worst. I cannot stand by while a rogue church leadership regime becomes complicit to their fabrications. There has been a grave injustice to mom and her family. I feel led in my heart and compelled to honor my responsibility, seeing so many hurt and brokenhearted congregants in my travels.

Misperceptions can be damaging and defeating. Memories can be effaced and short at times. Generalities can be often deceiving as appearances. I believe my mother has helped many people, just as she has broken countless hearts. I have talked with those who have left the Tabernacle Church over the inner circle's uncultured behavior and mom's unyielding doctrines. There are scores of believers and nonbelievers that have been led to the understanding that our mother has been mistreated by her children. Then there are those with a poor understanding as to how a mother could treat her children so defectively.

Children are not responsible for the actions of their parents. Generalities and vagueness can be misinterpreted and lead to confusion.

We have a stronger memory of how we are treated and reminisce less about what people say to us. From my research, extreme legalism does not have a place in churches, families, or a role in individual lives. The personality of extreme legalism can be obstructive to God's sheep. Whether your own legalistic ideas or the church's extreme rules and ideology, both result in broken hearts, broken church relationships with a diminished church membership. Church congregations need rules and guidelines for their existence. However, when pastors fear losing control of their congregations, those rules become extreme, leading to one's own self-doctrines. It creates a dangerous environment that does not serve God, Christianity, or any of us well. There is a far better approach and a better way than the ideology of extreme legalism. I challenge ministers to build God's churches on God promises, not on manufactured church drama or man-made agendas. People's well-being are essential, and above all, what we do and say is paramount to God. Let me just say, I am by no means generalizing all churches to be on a watch list, nor am I categorizing all churches as evil. The fact is when we know better, we can do better.

God has given me the strength, the wisdom, and courage of my convictions to say mom's family drama is *disingenuous* and *forged.* The unobvious does not become obvious until it is expressively obvious. Somebody has to step up to say, "Stop the madness and devastation!" Doing what's truthful is sometimes a result of "Going against the grain."

> Although the Lord sent prophets to the people to bring them back to him, and though they testified against them, they would not listen. Then the spirit of God came upon Zachariah son of Jehoiada the priest. He stood before the people and said, "This is what God says: 'Why do you disobey the Lord's commands? You will not prosper. Because you have forsaken the Lord, he has forsaken you. But they plotted against him, and by order of the king they stoned him to death in the courtyard of the Lord's temple. King Joash did not remember the kindness Zachariah's father Jehoiada had shown him but killed his son who said as he lay

dying, "May the Lord see this and call you to account."
(2 Chronicles 24:19–22 NIV)

This is not a pleasant position for any child to be in. However, the record of accusations and presumptions is in need of repair with injections of truth and fact. Our family predicament has been an unending conflict. It is time to straighten up an old score. The only way out of this family crisis is through the front door. There is no back door to go out from this tangled web of deception. Mother emboldened and allowed her church leadership regime to mistreat her family and then rewarded those that do with a nod of admiration, gifts, or money.

"Darkness cannot drive out darkness. Only light can do that." (Martin Luther King Jr.)

The inner circle that holds Mother's ladder has victimized our mom and her family to deceptive devices, which is no less than an unlawful family hijacking or relative to a historical biblical stoning. I, my sister, and brother want to see things done morally and ethically. Some church leadership regimes have fallen short on principled codes of conduct. For some reason I thought we were aiming higher when it came to a moral responsibility of how we conduct ourselves. This goes beyond our personal feelings of how we remember being mistreated by others.

When we called the corporate leadership regime out on their misbehavior, Mom and the inner circle turned their attention to a relentless quest to destroy her children's creditability. This crusade to satisfy their lustful desire continued for years and goes on still today. As I matured, regrettably mom pretended to the public and congregants that she has always reached out to her children and that we have rejected her as our mother. But behind closed doors mom was ridiculing us while all the while she and the leadership regime were pushing us out of her church.

Our family drama rides on a string of deceptive stories riddled with unclear facts manufactured by mom and the church leadership regime. I believe some congregants do not know how to stop this ride to get off. What is one to do in this case? The congregants, just as the family members, have no back door from these situations. They are caught in a paradigm of pride and denial. Sad to say, most of the Tabernacle Church congregants don't feel empowered to challenge the drama. They just go with the flow. Then there are those who are in it for what they can get out of it. The inner circle left no room for reconciliation for this man-made drama. It is not our strength that kept us whole and somewhat stable but the strength of God through us. mom and the inner circle continue their efforts in casting the pastor's children in a negative light. This in itself is an offense to God and a direct attack on the fabric of family values. Family values are not complicated and should be fairly easy to understand for believing churchgoers.

I was the recipient of the Dr. Martin Luther King Humanitarian Award. Some of mom's congregants also heard the exciting news. I had a person from the Tabernacle Church call me, saying, "I would love to attend the humanitarian award ceremony, but the pastor might show up and find me there thinking I might be in support of you. I am afraid to come there."

I sent mom an e-mail inviting her to the humanitarian awards ceremony. She responded twice to the invitation. It was almost as if she had to be reprogrammed by the leadership regime that I was supposed to be the adversary and not her oldest son who loved her. Take a look at our exchange:

Hello Ma,

Wishing you the best in the New Year with many blessings. I will be the recipient of an award on January 17. The award is the humanitarian award. If you are interested in attending, please let me know.

Love,
James Jr."

Date: Wed, 12 Jan 2011 05:42:36
From: Mom@xxx.com
Subject: Congratulations!
To: Jayalston@xxx.com

Happy New Year, James, I wouldn't mind attending, but on the 17th I am on the program for the late

Martin Luther King service. What is the time of your event? Thanks for the invitation and I hope it be joyous for you and the rest.

Love Ma

P.S. Thanks for the lovely Christmas card.

A week later I received the second response out of the clear blue from Mother:

Date: Wed, 19 Jan 2011 19:36:29

From: Mom@xxx.com
Subject: RE: Invitation
To: Jayalston@xxx.com

Hello James

How did your day go for receiving your reward? Again thanks for the invitation, but I found your insulting words on mine, saying if I am interested. I am always interested for you to do well and be blessed by the mercies of God. I feel you should have sent me an invitation, leaving out "if I am interested." I am sure no one else had those words on their invitation. Also I didn't know if you wanted me there. If you decide to invite me to any more of your functions, just send me a decent invitation like everybody else's OK! Did you put those words there to keep me away? Don't read anything negative into this e-mail. I am not upset, just need some understanding. I am used to dealing with rejection. God has given me victory in that area. I always wish you well and do pray for you. The woman, who caused you to be who you are.

Love Ma

After reading mom's second e-mail, it was implicit those around mom were not lying dormant. I had seen this kind of work before. This obstructionist work had the signature and hallmark of Tessy or Melvin. Melvin was a young lad when he came into the Tabernacle Church one evening saying his grandmother Ruthie had hit him in the head with a hammer and he could not go back home to her. Mother believed him and took him into our home. His grandmother became upset with Mother's accusations and the separation from her grandson. Melvin and his grandmother had an estranged relationship leading into the last moments to her life. She held to her story saying, "Melvin was not being truthful." From the time he moved in with our family, mom became his parent and church counsel. He advanced quickly, becoming a youth minister under Mother's tutelage.

During my teenage years, Melvin and I had nothing in common. It struck me that he could be a cowardly and underhanded person. Mom would try to force me to spend time with him, but she was not always successful in gaining my cooperation. We had far different interests. I was into my music, being with friends, athletics, cars, girls, etc. His interest was predominately church and things that the girls and ladies were doing. Over the years Melvin and I never made a connection to having an authentic friendship. As adults Melvin and I had somewhat of a congenial relationship. He invited me and my sister to his apartment one evening. After watching him drink heavily, he admitted that he had engaged in behavior that would be unacceptable by church standards.

One admission he made that evening was when he said, "Mom has been saying and doing things behind you-all's back ever since I can remember." He went on to say, "You all were never in a position to see it. The rest of the church saw it." This led him to say, "Mom slapped me in the church for something I did not do. She is crazy. But she listens to me now." Melvin told us, "You have to know how to deal with mom by telling her what she wants to hear. And I learned to do that." He continued by saying, "Mom does and says what she wants. It's her church." In growing up Melvin informed me he was jealous of our family because he felt neglected and abandoned by his parents. Becoming a member of the Tabernacle Church gave him a sense of belonging. After college, Melvin severed his relationship from the church. He would attend services once or twice per year. However, he kept his hand in the family by his influence, showering mom with disingenuous nonstop praise. He managed to maintain a relationship with her by visiting often while helping her with computer work and having dinner on a regular basis. Melvin's field of study was psychology. He maintained notes, charts, logs, and graphs on his computer about our family. We became the subjects for his doctorial dissertation, but he was unable to complete the challenges of the program.

Melvin spoke to me often by telephone in the 1990s when he was struggling in his workplace. Concerning the Tabernacle he would say, "Their way of worship is way too crazy." However, he maintained closeness to mom, borrowing money for his financial support. On January 28, 2013, mother asked me to drive her to the Hackensack Hospital psychiatric unit where Melvin had been admitted. He was taken there by his close friend who had been uneasy for some time by his conduct and behavior at work. Because he is a counselor in Rockland County, she thought it best to drive him to New Jersey for help.

Melvin said he was hearing voices, telling the doctors at the hospital that these voices were saying someone was going to murder him. He had purchased a shotgun as the voices were telling him snipers were on his roof. The police came to his residence on several occasions in response to 911 calls made by him. Each time they found no evidence of snipers. When I visited him at the hospital, he told me he had been sitting in a chair every night with the shotgun he purchased. My brother pointed out to us that this has been going on for a while. Steven said, "If someone was going to take him out, wouldn't they have done so by now?" Melvin had provided Mother with some names of people whom he thought might be after him if he should turn up missing. I felt a compassion for him that I thought by no means would have ever happened.

There were often times my sister would ask of me and our brother a rhetorical question: "What is wrong with the people? What kind of people are they?" Meanwhile other congregants would be saying, "Poor pastor having to put up with, and pastor, these people. It is not Pastor. It's the people." Tessy would often smirk, saying, "They take the chair off Pastor's back and replaced it with a table." Then Tessy would say, "The bus pulls right up to the Tabernacle Church door and lets them out right here." Tessy would quietly say that in the office she could hear the screws loosely rattling around in some of the parishioners' heads as they would walk away from her desk. I wasn't sure what all of that meant, except it was not positive.

I have chosen my words carefully and said, "There is no way God would *not* fix our family problems if they existed through prayer and professional counseling." The problem is there is no problem. The family has been hoodwinked, running around in a circle scratching our heads *not* for years but *decades*. Mother built her ministry and church on the sacrifice of her children's reputation, not knowing how, or wanting to repair what she and the inner circle had broken. There are times that your reputation is all you have to define a value to what kind of person you are. Having a good character and being true to your words are strong attributes for anyone. Having these qualities under a personal attack for no reason is ungodly and insulting. Our vision was obscured while we battled the storm for our reputations, not knowing what we were up against. The brunt of the storm came when we understood and learned of the intent of the leadership regime. The leadership regime had a continuum to create and maintain trouble and raging storms in our lives. They had no intention to make anything we did count or leave us with any creditability. Mom went into unchartered waters dragging her children through the mud, encouraged by a uncaring church corporate leadership regime. Mom, not seeing a way to hold on to her own creditability, made the decision to sacrifice her children as her way out. Mother convinced her congregation and friends that she was the best mother in the world. Many of mom's new arriving congregants to the Tabernacle Church would say, "I wish you were my mother." I never heard anyone, on their way out of the double doors with the intent to never return, say, "I wish you were my mother."

FAMILY AND CHURCHES

AFTER MANY YEARS OF TEARS, sorrow, misunderstandings, and brokenheartedness, God made the confusion clear. Only He could have brought us out of the storms to safe harbor. Here is a philosophical approach I used in church and business. In this life we are either in a problem, headed to a problem, or coming out of a problem. This is the cycle of life's challenges and the carrying of our crosses. Mom stomped around for years riding her emotional propaganda of rejection and drama on her children's psyche and in our hearts as we searched and looked to God for remedies. Mom never offered up a solution in the years of crisis. The crisis was the crisis that never was.

Mom's remedy to this manufactured family crisis was to clearly place her children into harm's way. Mom said, "You all should go to the Iraq war." Our mother made use of family time by telling us we all needed to be saved and needed to get right with God's church. In public, most times the words from mother's mouth were smooth as butter; however, in her heart she harbored war. Those thought out to be the devil or against her doctrines became a target for assault by her inner circle. Mom's favorite scripture and commonly quoted to her dwindling congregation was "No weapon forged against you will prevail, and you will refute every tongue that accuses you" (Isaiah 54:17 NIV). Mother used this scripture to unite people's emotions for her cause. This expressive cry out from mom caused emotions to overflow and enslaved folks to believing the church was under attack by some type of physical or evil forces incessantly. She maintains absolute control over her parishioner's minds and thought process. In order to be or maintain membership at the Tabernacle Church, you must submit yourself to mother 100 percent. The measurement of submission is by strict obedience and loyalty to her will. And of course your financial contribution measures your sacrifice and dedication to mother.

When a congregant departed the Tabernacle Church expressing their discontent with mom and the leadership regime, the leadership without apprehension would make their departure a painful process. Most congregants knew of the process and ridicule that departing members faced. Fueled by a gang mentality the leadership regime would launch smear campaigns against a departing member. Congregants feared the risk of their reputation being tarnished by mom and the church leadership. Parishioners dissolved their church membership by making up excuses that they had to return back to their country or relocate to another state, county, or a city that required further travel. Some would leave in a fit of rage and argument. Others would just dissolve and disappear never to be heard from again.

Mom and her inner circle have conducted themselves in such a dysfunctional fashion I was led in my heart to talk with a professional doctor and therapist. After my visit, I made an appeal to mom and the family. I told mom that I had a professional therapist on standby. Her name is Dr. Alice Plummer who was the director of a Christian hospital in Wyckoff, New Jersey, which is twenty-five minutes away. I explained to mom that Dr. Plummer is a medical doctor and psychiatrist. Mom refused my offer, telling me she would only go through a family counselor if they were a minister. Mom chose a preacher from Atlanta, Georgia, that would have been acceptable to her. The preacher was a regular visitor to the Tabernacle Church, who usually departed after preaching with pockets full of congregants' tithe and offerings.

My sister became suspect and said "No thanks" to mom's idea. My sister recommended that we visit with a professional with no history to mom and our family. I agreed as my brother also did. Mom was insistent the only way she would go forward would have to be on her terms. After this mom said this, leaving no alternatives, the counseling sessions were banished without further options.

One of the biggest fallacies of the leadership regime was to subject congregants to deception, all in the name of Jesus. There was no family crisis *or problems to be fixed.* It was an inverted story, a myth, a tale out of school. Often I would hear Lesley say to the unsuspecting when mom would embarrass and humiliate people in her flock: "If you can take it, you can make it." The newer church generation will not accept or understand Lesley's antic. They will be visitors quick to go right back out of the church door. The Y generations are no longer mystified by man-made drama. It is a new day. Our younger generation are not easily tricked or fooled. The new millennium is a high-tech society, astute to the world and global affairs, and churches must stand for a purpose in their lives. No longer are people looking to get on a misguided church ark. They will build an ark of their own first.

I thought about this passage in the Bible:

> Don't let anyone deceive you in any way, for that day will not come until the rebellion occurs and the man of lawlessness is revealed, the man doomed to destruction. He will oppose and will exalt himself over everything that is called God or is worshiped, so that he sets himself up in God's temple, proclaiming himself to be God. (2 Thessalonians 2:3–4 NIV)

Mom and the inner circle have no intentions of fixing their manufactured melodrama. Mom's melodrama became her truth, which caused her to crusade against her family and others that were non-supportive to her nonfactual allegations, unnatural behaviors, and negative propaganda. Some congregants feel they have invested too much of themselves. They have put their sweat, blood, time, and money in the Tabernacle Church and would look foolish to try and upright the ship.

The Tabernacle cannot afford to pay the price to end what they have manufactured and produced for years. The product produced by the leadership regime was morally reprehensible from the start—well, before being served down to the congregants and brought to the public square. There is a downside by suppressing the truth in order to deceive, and that is the loss of creditability to the Word of God. Not to mention the negative impact to the example of family principles and values. The Bible makes reference for us to occupy until he comes. Will church organizations and leadership regimes have a role in people falling away from God's Word and becoming nonbelievers in churches in the latter day? Will churches be able to hold their own through strong moral values and biblical principles of God's divine grace? There are church leadership regimes whose very existence in the way they handle themselves is an offense to mankind.

This very situation has profoundly shaken our family's faith in church leadership regimes. I, my sister, and my brother along with mom's grands were pushed out of the Tabernacle Church by an uncaring church leadership regime. The church corporate leadership evicted the pastor's children from the Tabernacle Church, principled on their ideology, enrobed with ungodly principles of grace. We were orphaned by a church corporate leadership regime that did not want us there. We put our lives in the hands of a church ministry that we thought was safe. We were diligent about working hard on the behalf of the ministry and the vision that mom said God gave her.

Today if I visit a church, mom would call me the very next day telling me the church I visited was nothing and not about God. Some pastors and members were bold enough to tell me what mom would say. I respect them for that. If I gave an offering in some churches, mom would call me, telling me how much I gave to that church. I stopped filling out tithe and offering envelopes because giving is something I take personally between God and me. Thank goodness for privacy. You know all those counseling sessions you thought were sacred and intimate. Well, besides Minister Lesley, his new wife Serika, Reverend Helen, Dosie, Tessy, and the Tabernacle inner circle, God only knows who else knows about your personal life and business.

One elder told me if you don't want your business out, don't tell the pastor. The same elder stood up in the pulpit on a Sunday morning worship service informing the congregants that the pastor would be the one to judge them with God on Judgment Day. The congregants agreed by answering back to him with "Amen, thank you, Jesus" and hallelujahs. When I heard this, I thought, *Is that biblical or made up out of ignorance to Bible fact?* Years later, the same elder rejected the way the Tabernacle leadership treated his son Shame, leaving the church in discord in early 2012.

When I found myself literally locked out of the Tabernacle Church and the Faith and Educational Center, I was saddened and disappointed by this punitive and brash unwarranted behavior. I took this as a symbolic message to say, "You are not welcome here!" I also thought about this, *Does Christ force himself into your life, or do you usher the spirit of Christ into your heart?* I heard a minister say these words, "Jesus does not go where he is not wanted." By no means am I saying I am Jesus, just to clear up the fact for the critical reader.

In July 2013, mom requested our support by accompanying her to an annual Prayer Day Service in Brooklyn, New York. The service was at the Renaissance Center of Pilgrim Assemblies International Incorporated. Mother was one of several platform speakers on that day. If I were to have written a press release about that day, it would have read like this:

> Church Leader Humiliates Family on Annual Prayer Day: A DVD went on sale July 18, 2013, of a church service that was purposely intended to humiliate a pastor's family. What was done to a family in the midst of a congregation of people was not done in the spirit of love. Paul emphasized in 1 Corinthians 13:13, "And now abides faith, hope, love, these three; but the greatest of these is Love."
>
> A bishop who holds the title of the house prophet picked up the microphone in front of the congregation then laid his right hand upon a woman's head—who is a pastor, mother, and grandmother— uttering statements that he said were from God. The self-proclaimed house prophet said to the pastor several times, "You will live a long life, and God is giving you a second wind." Then the bishop went

on to say, "There are people lingering around you waiting for your ministry to fail, but that's not going to happen. God is going to deal with those family members. They think that they are getting an inheritance, but they will not because your ministry belongs to God. And the devil will not have it."

We sat defenseless in the choir seats behind the ministers facing the congregants while the bishop berated us with his forecast. After Bishop Shorts realized mom's family was present, he cowardly ran away and off the pulpit. Steven was so distressed over the Shorts forecast that he left his seat to leave from the church. Just before he got up to leave, he looked to me with tears in his eyes, saying, "James, I am done, I am done, I am so done…" Later in the week Steven drove back to Brooklyn to purchase copies of the DVD for all of us. After viewing the DVD, sadly, it was precisely what Bishop Shorts said! The bishop implicated mom's children and grands were of the devil and we were wishing harm to come upon our mother. In my embarrassment, this bishop knew nothing about us. What kind of bishop and church corporation allows this kind of conduct to go on, and why?

I began to think about people and families who are subjected to this kind of maltreatment in the church. Some churchgoers are being misled into thinking that church abuse is an act of God, allowing this unacceptable behavior to go unchallenged. People sacrifice to get to church and support their leaders. They sacrifice their time, and liberal giving, only to be shortchanged in return when leadership regimes use their position of power to publicly humiliate and verbally abuse them.

We have not been lingering around our mother to see what we can get as a result of her death but rather spending time with her to become the family that God has intended us to be. We were in a process. After a thorough review of the DVD on sale to the public, on July 23, 2013, the Alston family requested a meeting with Archbishop Brown, the president of Pilgrim Assemblies Inc., along with Bishop Shorts.

The family's request for a meeting and to have our voice heard went unanswered by the Pilgrim Assemblies Inc. We were told by Diane, who is the archbishop's secretary, that the archbishop and Shorts would be in contact with us for a meeting or a conference call every week. To no justification, her promises were broken every week. We had no voice and remain to be insignificant to the Pilgrim Assemblies Incorporated. Pilgrims Assemblies has cowardly gone off into the night under cover. Our requests continue to be ignored by Bishop Brown and Shorts for no explanation.

Mom says, "I didn't hear what Bishop Shorts said. I was in the spirit. I can't get involved. I have never spoken negatively about my family to Bishop Shorts or anyone else." This unjustifiable prophecy placed our family into the hurl of division and family discord once again another setup by a church leadership regime. Our family once again felt pretty beat up by a pulpit bully. Years of unprotected family values took its toll and caused division in our relationship with our mother. Unbeknown to Bishop Shorts we had recently started working on reconciling our family differences. The Tabernacle Church leadership publicly says, "The children are always welcome." Needless to say the spiritual and natural door has never been unlocked. The situation manufactured by the Tabernacle's inner circle leadership has served no one well. The Tabernacle Church leadership regime, by their own design, has left little to no reconciliation means to congregants. If church experiences have left you feeling irreverent to God's divine grace and feeling irrelevant to the promises of God's Word, there is a higher power to mend those broken hearts from church experiences. Cherish your family, love one another! Be heedful when family separation stands knocking at your door. Acknowledge it, but don't embrace it with a callous attitude.

There are times we make the people who care about us cry. We cry for those who never care for us. And we care for those who will never cry for us. This is true of life. It's strange, yet true. It's never too late to let a family member or friends know you care and love them. Help others to make it right, and fix it! Life is short.

20

THE UNFORGETTABLE STORM

THIS CHAPTER IS DEDICATED TO Steven, my brother, and is a tribute to his survival of the unforgettable storm. Steven was last to be baptized with the distasteful and repugnant opposition of mom. I could have dedicated this chapter to any one of us, including parishioners who have come forward to share their personal stories. Steven's experiences within the church and its leadership regime are symbolic to many. Some leadership regimes have placed churches into troublesome spots due to their antics and pretense. It is very difficult to defend yourself from what you cannot see or you are not suspect of.

Mom's youngest of children, Steven, bore the physical and mental fury of the unsuspecting wrath harbored inside mom's heart. Earlier I talked about Steven serving his country in the first Gulf War under the commander and Chief George H. W. Bush. Steven was blessed to arrive home with some physical ailments from the war; however, thanks be to God he arrived back without being maimed. As large or small as it may seem, the United States Military protects our way of life in America. This gives us the rights we have, especially when it comes to worship. Far too often we take our liberty for granted by glazing over the value and appreciation of what we are so blessed to have, our freedoms. Please join me and my family in thanking Steven and the military for their valor and dedication to the service of the greatest country on earth. I have taken notice over the years. Steven appears to uphold Christianity and his personal belief in the Bible. Little did Steven know or understand, upon arriving back home, he was going to be challenged with family conflict that periled the Gulf War. One of God's greatest securities is feeling and knowing you have emotional safety within your loved ones. What happened between mother and Steven was inexcusable and is not biblically principled. There are times when you must let people stand on your shoulders when you are the stronger. I have always promoted fair play by not kicking someone when they are down but extended a hand to help them get up and onto their feet. I have been fortunate to know some wonderful people in my travels that were respectful, well respected, with abundant wisdom, understanding, and smarts. The question has been posed to me many times, what happened between your mom and your brother?

The time has come and a venue for Steven to talk of his personal climatic discord between his mother and him. It saddens me as to what happened, but I have been blessed with the opportunity to be the means to help upright the ship from the past. To do this correctly, Steven divests himself of his past with mom by saying this, "After having the Rockland County sheriff 's department escort me out of mom's front door, all based on a false report, I was left with no money and no shelter. I was devastated. Thinking through things, I couldn't understand. mom and I sat down and talked about me needing to find my own place because we were not living in peace. I was certain that I could find a place within three months.

"Leading up to the false order of protection, I was often bothered by mom's negative comments to me in front of her parishioners, and I told her so. We both knew it was time for me to leave. A week after our conversation and agreement, I was awakened at 3:00 a.m. and escorted out by police. I called a friend, told her what happened, and she said, 'Come on over.' When I got to her place, she came outside, in the snow, hugging me with tears in her eyes. My friend knew of my character and reputation. She couldn't understand why my mother would have the police escort me out of the house during a snowstorm with no place to go. She told me that I could stay at her house overnight.

"I am not the kind of man that would ask to sleep in a woman's bed if we're not married, so I slept on the couch. Working for the church and for my mother left me underemployed and underpaid. Not having much money while working for the church, I went to the bank after remembering that my mother put a large sum of cash in a safety deposit box with both our names on it. Later I understood she put the money under my name to hide it from the Internal Revenue Service in order to not pay income taxes. When I got to the bank, mother had already removed the money from the safety deposit box. Mom knew I had no funds and the bank would be the first place I would go. Now I was dead broke, but thanks to my friend I did have shelter at her home. She told me that I could stay with her as long as I needed to. One night turned into six months.

"My friend is a registered nurse who at the time started a new job and a new life since her husband had recently left her for another woman. Her new job involved working late evenings. Since she trusted me with her children, I took on the role of being a male figure, responsible for making a positive and lasting impact in the lives of her two boys. I was there to make sure they went to bed on time. In the middle of the night when they couldn't sleep or got sick, I was there for them. I made sure they arrived at school on time, picked them up at the end of the day, helped them with their homework, school projects, papers, and studies. I ensured they consumed healthy meals, we worked out, played basketball and football, they were taught the basics of karate, which is a good way to grow discipline in youngsters.

"I advised and counseled them about life, took them to Sunday school and church when their mother was assigned to work on weekends. I answered their questions about God and life in the best way that I could and so much more. By doing all of this their mother could work double shifts and overtime. She was able to shore up her financial base as a single parent and household provider for her boys. It worked out, so I had shelter and was able to make a strong contribution to the development of her two young sons, and that was rewarding for me after my own devastation. I'm not a parent, but I got a good taste of what parents feel when they invest time and love into their kids. It's an experience that I will never forget. Within six months I was able to move to secure a job and into my own apartment.

"At a later date my friend reconciled with her husband, which was a blessing for both of them. I'm grateful to God that I was able to find a way to make good of a bad situation. "I caution the readers of this submission to never allow yourself to be in a position to have your livelihood controlled by any one person, which includes family members.

"After finishing my master's degree, I became established in the state of Virginia but left it all behind and moved to New York. I love my mother and wanted to see her peacefully enjoy her latter years. Mother kept promising me that she was going to renovate the walk-in basement to an apartment with my own entry. I did what mom had requested of me and what I had promised, and that was to assist and help with the operations of the church.

"My brother James and sister Pamela warned me of her unintentional broken promises and what would actually happen. They knew that in a matter of time she would turn and eventually turn her parishioners against me because that's what happened to them. Unfortunately, I didn't believe my siblings, as she consistently called and expressed how much she needed me to come home and help because James and Pamela left her high and dry. Eventually I began feeling resentful and disappointed in my siblings for leaving our mother in this predicament. I returned to New York, moved in to my mother's home, and eventually like my two siblings became a target for her mistreatment.

"I learned so much from this horrific experience. After being thoroughly warned by my brother and sister, I found myself in the path of discord with mom. They could have turned their back on me and said 'I told you so' but they never did. My brother and sister helped me in the time of need. They made themselves available as well as their resources, spending time with me to ensure that I didn't sink into deep depression. I'm forever grateful to God for giving me an older brother and sister to be there in my hardest time ever and my friend who took me in."

It was a long and rough storm for Steven, brought on by the hands of an uncaring and insensitive church leadership regime. I have asked God many days how could people be so insensitive to other humans, let alone their pastor's begotten children. I am not the judge; however, the cost and pain associated with abuse and merciless treatment of anyone is absolutely objectionable. And for those that stand by condoning, abetting, and aiding in this conduct without guilt, it's shameful!

This indecency came on the heels of serving his country and the betterment of himself by earning his master's degree. Let me conclude by saying that Steven is an ordained minister.

21

WHAT? WHO, ME?

WHO, ME? WHAT? WHY DO I have to apologize? Why am I always the one who's apologizing? What did I do to you? I didn't do anything? I am not going back! Do these words sound proverbial, words that we have grown used to hearing? An apology is a written or spoken expression of one's regret, remorse, or sorrow for having insulted, failed, injured, or wronged another person. Life opens the door to our human side, granting us hundreds of opportunities for giving and receiving apologies throughout our lifetime. "And forgive us our debts, as we also have forgiven our debtors" (Matthew 6:11–13 NIV). "Yet now I am happy, not because you were made sorry, but because your sorrow led you to repentance. For you became sorrowful as God intended and so were not harmed in any way by us" (2 Corinthians 7:8–10 NIV).

We all want to look in the mirror and see someone we respect, someone who acts with honor and integrity. "Apology is a lovely perfume; it can transform the clumsiest moment into a gracious gift," says author Margaret Lee Runbeck. I was given an apology by Minister Lesley on one occasion, by saying, "Forgive me for what you said I did to you." I actually felt this apology would have been less offensive by not having any apology at all. I have often thought about this, *Is a somewhat halfhearted apology better than no apology at all?* If you're apologizing to avoid further trouble or to please someone else, chances are you did not feel you did anything wrong and the person is insignificant to you.

Working in corporate America for over thirty years, I learned that giving a timely and appropriate apology is serious for a business and a powerful tool to be empowered by. Outside of professional business etiquette, the ability to give somebody a deserving apology is an awesome display of reconciliation. A sincere apology is clout for a leader in business if you use it correctly. As important to the country's moral fabric as an apology has been, alarming to me is how lackadaisical churches are in teaching how to give a sincere apology to one another.

You must reflect to regret. When you allow yourself to be reflective, you can then be regretful and apologetic. The precipitation for an effective apology starts with the willingness of usually two people. Two things people must be willing to do in order to start on the road to an effective apology are the following: First, the person giving the apology understands the harm they have caused by their action to another person or persons. Second, the person receiving the apology is willing to listen and accept what the apologizer has to say in their own words. One other important point is asking a person for an apology. If you have been truly offended by a person's action or wronged, ask them for an apology. If they refuse, do not harbor ill feeling toward their unwillingness. Go on with your life and ask God to forgive them. And above all, ask God to give you a forgiving heart toward that person. Most folks are unacquainted with how to offer an affective apology. Above all learn to forgive yourself! "Jesus said, 'Father, forgive them, for they do not know what they are doing'" (Luke 23:34 NIV). Keep in mind, I wrote earlier, "Hurting people hurt people."

Church corporate leadership regimes have lost sight of modeling the basic concept and value of a sincere apology. They are missing a great opportunity with their busy agendas by not teaching congregants how to give an effective apology to each other. The art of an effective apology is needed in today's world, and churches have the platform to inspire parishioners to sincerely understand how to apologize to one another. I listened attentively every first Sunday to ministers garbed in their white robes talking to their flocks dressed in a sea of white, telling them before communion that you don't want to have communion to be damnation to your soul. After which they would instruct the congregants to remove themselves from their seats, go around the church asking the other to forgive them while they hugged and cried on each other's shoulders. After this, congregants are allowed to take part in the communion service. I never quite understood why I was asking a stranger to forgive me, and then, them me. Not knowing what they had done to me or me knowing what I had done to them. But I did what I was instructed to do without question. I believe communion is a spiritual provision to awaken our sense to the significance of forgiving and apologizing. I ask a rhetorical question, Would it be difficult to devote some Bible Study teachings on how to give a meaningful and effective apology? "Apology is the willingness to value the relationship more than the need to be right," says John Kador, author of *Effective Apology*. If your only reason to apologize is because you got caught, you are not nearly ready to apologize. When you apologize to someone, you're going to need to be able to discuss it. Be sure you can describe your actions clearly and you are ready to be honest. When people cannot apologize for a wrong, they may consider themselves scorekeeper of the game, and an apology defines their winning or losing. There are four things that come to the forefront with the inability of a sincere apology:

(1) They may deny any wrongdoing. (2) They may not know how to apologize, which becomes their responsibility to learn how. (3) The person involved is insignificant to them; they don't care about the relationship. (4) They feel they are above reproach, having no accountability to anyone.

There are times when insensitivity allows a sincere apology to expire, moving into a position to say "too little too late" where just an apology is not enough anymore. With a sincere apology comes the opportunity for reconciliation between parties. Lack of a real, sincere, trustworthy apology creates wars that last for years from buildup of resentment and hurt, ruining many lives and relationships, personal and business. Apologizing resets the clock, allowing the healing process to begin.

Most of us have difficulty admitting when we are wrong. We are more prone to pointing out when we feel offended. Sometimes apologies are made with blame to the other person (e.g., "You should have told me" or "You should have said something before now"). I have heard this as an escape door from wrongdoing: "You are the reason I behaved the way I did. You made me mad. That is why I did what I did to you." A person giving a sincere apology shoulders the responsibility for a wrong. There is an art to giving a sincere apology to a person other than saying, "Sorry!" or some other impertinent remark as to say, "Get over it."

To give a sincere apology there needs to be an expression of empathy. You must let the person being apologized to know that you understand their pain and what they have had to endure. As the saying goes, walk a mile in my moccasins before placing judgment. Spend time understanding how a person feels and the circumstances they are in. Sometimes you might have to say, "I have no excuse for what I said or did." A sincere apology is not something you do while walking briskly past a person. Be sure your apology is straightforward. Don't dance around the crust and use hedging techniques that come across as being disingenuous.

An apology should be meaningful, personal, and sometimes privately done. At other times depending on what has happened, the apology might have to be done in a public forum in order to fix what has been broken. Your apology should include three important ingredients: (1) regret and empathy, (2) responsibility, (3) remedy. It is normal to feel some guilt when you give a sincere apology. You are in an honest frame of mind.

It is very tough to talk yourself out of a situation that you purposely walked yourself into. It is good to give people the space and time to forgive as well. We all mend differently physically and spiritually. Family members that are closely relationship may need to go the extra mile with a sincere apology and forgiveness by doing what it takes within reason. Enlist an agreement for a behavioral change so it does not happen again, or keep happening over and over.

Here are two modules of interactive people skills you can use in your daily interaction with people. The first is an acronym called LISTEN, and the second is called START. To help with listening to a person who is trying to tell you how they feel out of anger and hurt: LISTEN.

L – Listen with your inner ear attentively.

I – Identify emotion. (Anger, disappointment, upset, etc.)

S – Search, to find remedial solutions.

T – Talk up in agreement.

E – Engage in commitment. (What will change to keep it from happening again?)

N – Next step. (Where do we go from here? Hug, handshake, bury the hatchet.)

After listening attentively, paraphrase what the person has said based on what you heard. This will improve the communication and understanding between both parties. This also allows ambiguities to be cleared up and restores the chance to identify real emotions without misconceptions between the parties, rekindling trust and confidence to move forward with each other. In some cases there is a clearly defined wrongdoer and a victim. However, there are instances where there is some blame on both parties. Receiving an apology is just as important to understanding that the person giving you an apology feels your hurt and pain. Allow them to speak uninterrupted. This will tell you if they are truly sincere and understand what you are feeling. Don't be upset if they miss some of the words that identify your feelings and emotions. After they are done, help them with the words describing how you feel. For example, you might say to them, "I was not disappointed. I was angry with you." The second easy acronym to remember is START.

S – Start the healing process, stating how you *felt before.*

T – Tell the person how you *feel now.*

A – Attend and respond to what you have heard.

R – Respond positively to a sincere apology. Don't reignite the offense.

T – Thank them. Acknowledge that you sincerely accept their apology.

Keep in mind these steps are just a beginning stage to understanding the art of giving a sincere apology to another person. These are skills that can be of practical use in your daily interaction with people.

At this time, I find it suitable to say to the churches' brokenhearted. We the pastor's children solitary say, "We're apologetic and understanding to your disappointments. We convey our deepest compassion to any pain you endured while in the care of any church leadership regime." There are times when church regimes are clueless to the damage and mayhem they create in their churches and among their congregants' lives. There is no acceptable excuse to their lack of knowledge to God's grace principles and mistreatment of God's flocks. You have to be big to forgive.

22

IN HONOR OF A FALLEN SOLDIER

I PUT PEN TO PAPER, fingers on the home keys of the keyboard. As I strike the keys, Andrea's face comes before me and is succinct to my mind. I remember our last interaction—the sincerity of her words and the enthusiasm in her voice. I am numb by the choice of a young woman living in the most advanced country in the world. She had the most modern day medicine and health care at her disposal. However, Andrea's unyielding efforts to show loyalty and faith to her church leadership regime placed her in a peerless time and situation with the clock running toward her demise.

Andrea Taylor-Benjamin left behind a young son and husband when she was overtaken by breast cancer. I, along with others, feel blessed and honored to have known Andrea (Dumpsey) over the years. Those that knew Andrea through her childhood called her Dumpsey. The nickname followed her into her adult life. Dumpsey was a Christian soldier that held allegiance to the Tabernacle Church Inc. She left us with questions that are unanswered and our minds are unable to grasp. She left a vacuum in our lives that we cannot explain as she departed this life leaving her crosses behind. I will forever remain confounded by the distinction and mental clarity of her choices. She was three years old when I met her. I remember her little matching outfit with black shiny shoes and turndown socks. She was cute as could be. Dumpsey had always had a wonderful disposition, full of joy and life, respectful and courteous to others. She had a persistence and toughness about her, yet she maintained politeness and good manners. As I stepped into the front door of the church, my first day to start my second time around, she met me in the hallway with a hug and smile. We had a quick exchange of greetings while we ogled each other with warm smiles. Dumpsey said, "Deacon Alston, I am so glad you are back. Tessy and Pastor told me to talk to you about my idea." Dumpsey said in her persistent style, "I have been asking Tessy about an ATM for a while. I have not gotten an answer from her yet." Before I could respond, she launched into her recital and proposal with excitement and enthusiasm. She went on to say, "I thought it would be a good idea to have an ATM machine in the hallway. It would make it more convenient for people to get money for special offerings, instead of going up the street to the bank's ATM." I listened attentively. I, overwhelmed by it all, said, "Okay, let me check into all of that. I am just getting here. I will speak to Tessy and the pastor about it." I continued with, "Meanwhile can you write up your proposal with the details and how much volume or traffic you think the ATM will generate from congregants." It was easy for me to see how enthralled she was in her zeal to help her church.

When I first spoke with her, I did not realize how ailing she was. We spoke on the telephone several times. After a while she began to tell me how on some days she could not get up from the couch to care for her young son after he arrived home from school. I listened to her carefully as she told me how she believed on God healing her. Dumpsey said, "Some days are very hard, but my pastor said that God was going to heal me, and I have faith that he will."

She told me her doctor had been pleading with her to have surgery, but she had refused. To the best of my understanding, she felt that having the surgery would diminish her faith in the Tabernacle ministry. She is one of the bravest Christians that I have met. She looked death in the face right up until her demise, standing firm as to what the ministry had prophesied to her. The Tabernacle Church supported the cold fact that

God was going to heal her. She made known to me that all she had to do was to take God at his word. Her last words to me were, "I am standing firm on the promise of what God said." I thought it to be benevolent of Andrea in the face of her fatal illness to be concerned about installing an ATM in the church hallway. My efforts along with others were too late in convincing Andrea to go forward with breast surgery.

The doctors informed the family surgery was no longer an option to prevent the inevitable. The cancer cells had spread too far. Andrea told me that her physician explained thoroughly the progression of her terminal illness. She said her doctor was animate and profound about her diagnosis and prognosis leading to her demise if she did not have the breast surgery two years earlier. What I found astounding is Reverend Helen had breast cancer surgery years prior. She and mom never sounded a word of warning concerning breast cancer awareness to the congregants. Mom and Reverend Helen sat in the pulpit harboring their secret from the public, the congregants. I could not but help to think what a wonderful testimony this would have been for women and men.

One of mom's key members was diagnosed with breast cancer in October 2013. This came right on the heels of the pastoral celebration. Ironically, October is the month that the nation is focused on awareness and breast cancer survivors. The Power of Pink started in 1985. One in eight or 12.3 percent will be diagnosed. This does not reflect the number of men that will be diagnosed. The Tabernacle never took the time to mention breast cancer in the month of October or in prior years. Mom's members and the few that knew of her condition were ordered to silence. Why? Because nothing considered dire was allowed to happen at the Tabernacle—unless they were the ones to pronounce determination on a person's destiny.

Mom was visibly annoyed after one of her hospital visits with Andrea. She came back saying, "Every time Dumpsey's doctor comes into her hospital room, he has something negative to say. Nobody wants to hear all that!" Andrea's death was premature due to her victimization to a church leadership regime. Andrea placed her life on the line and into the hands of a church leadership regime's prediction that her outcome would be victorious. Andrea was courageous, staying the course, and stood her ground with what her church leadership regime said. I will always be haunted by the fact if Dumpsey felt she made the best choice when it became too late to do anything about her condition. There came a time and point in Andrea's life that there was truly no return, or reverse of decision to see her young son grow up.

Andrea's husband picked up his son and left the church heartbroken after her death. The husband had to figure out how to give Andrea an appropriate burial without beneficiary entitlement. Andrea's ex-husband was the beneficiary of her death policy and refused to assist the husband or son. He felt it was not his problem. During her illness, Andrea was more concerned about her church rather than preparing her paperwork naming her son and husband as the beneficiary to her death policy. The church leadership regime broke no laws, nor was responsible for any misconduct. Andrea made her choices. However, I question the moral responsibility of what happened. I believe churches should aim for a higher moral liability to their flocks and congregants. There was some confusion at the end of Andrea's death. Mom and the church leadership regime were saying in their circles that no one told Dumpsey to not take her medicine or follow the doctor's orders. Some congregants left the church after this statement. After listening to some concerns and hearing information here and there, I carefully weighed in with my thoughts.

I reiterated that Andrea had made her choices of free will, knowing that the outcome could be fatal. However, she was influenced by a church leadership regime that she had put absolute faith in. On the other hand, why didn't one of the church leadership members take on the responsibility to place her into one of their cars and insist she go for the surgery? I do not believe for one minute that the leadership conspired or expected Andrea to expire. But confined to their cowardly ignorance they sat and watched this young lady, their sister soldier, slowly drift to her death. No one stood up for Andrea and pleaded that enough is enough!

Now in the aftermath, Christians walk around finger-pointing and running away from what should have been their moral responsibility to Andrea. Some say she lacked faith. The woman went to her death. How much faith does it take? Let's be reasonable if there is such a thing. This kind of unawareness and perverse ideology is treacherous. By the time I walked back into the Tabernacle Church, time had run out for

Andrea. Upon her death, I wept, saying to myself, if I had only known much earlier how sick she was, maybe I could have convinced her into surgery. Andrea placed absolute 100 percent of her faith into a leadership regime that let her down. Her words to me were the pastor, the church leadership, and other leaders said, "God was going to heal me."

I, among many, was left heartbroken over Andrea's death. I write this chapter in honor of Andrea for being a brave, faithful, and loyal Christian soldier. Within two months into my arrival, for the second time around at the Tabernacle Church, Andrea was gone from our lives. Andrea and her family will not be forgotten.

With so many pop-up churches and existing churches, I thought this to be a necessary and fair question. I asked Steven, who is an ordained minister by mother, for his thoughts on the challenge of life-and-death decisions: How does a pastor or minister counsel an individual or their families in similar situations as Andrea had faced? Steven said, "James, this raises an honest question that will serve to challenge any pastor about congregant's personal life-and-death decisions. I don't think that anyone can say to another, including Pastors, that God said he is going to heal you of this deadly disease and the person take that as gospel. I believe if God speaks that to the person and the pastor says the same thing, then it is a confirmation of what God has already decreed.

"I'm glad that Church Incorporated goes beyond the surface to help people look deeper at issues that we were told not to talk about because it would be speaking against God's mouthpiece. I don't believe that there is a person on earth who can truthfully call themselves God's mouthpiece. I do believe when God speaks to our hearts or even gives a prophetic word to a prophet, it usually comes in the form of an image, concept, dream, vision, or strong sensation, not so much word for word. Prophecies are the confirmation of what God has already revealed. Those revelations can come in many different forms, but I believe that if God doesn't reveal it somehow first, then a person will put their faith in the messenger and not the supreme source of where the message came from."

I admonish and encourage congregants to rely on the advice and wisdom of your physician to assist in your healing process if need be. I see no sin or lack of faith in your decision to do so. I strongly recommend that you review your living will or departure will thoroughly, and it is current at all times, for the sake of your family and others. A house in order is easier to manage than a house in disarray. I understand people change their wills at particular moments based on their emotions, being upset, or mental instability. God's grace principles are clear in the Bible when it comes to wills and inheritance. In 2011 mom had an usher who testified to the congregants that she had a serious heart problem. Her testimony captivated the congregants by telling everyone that the doctors diagnosed her condition to be serious enough to be fatal to her health. The leadership regime prophesied to her condition, telling the congregants she would be healed by God. The usher came back after the leadership regime prayed over her, making claim that her specialist no longer saw the heart problem. This was after surgery and on a follow-up visit to the specialist's office. She told mom and the congregants that the pastor's prayers healed her and her heart problem had vanished.

Ultimately, she misled mom and the congregants to believe that her pastor's prayers and the prophecy she received was her only means to her being a walking miracle, never bringing up the cardiovascular surgery. All the while, her close friend and confidant, who is one of the pastor's closest adjutants, drove her to New York City for the heart surgery and retrieved her a few days after. Speaking to my mother she was unaware of the usher having been in the hospital. After informing mom of what I knew, mom directed her anger to me, saying in a condescending tone, "I thank you for telling me that. I didn't know. I went by what that girl was telling me."

I implore congregants to be respectful of your pastor and minister by not calling for them to walk on water. I believe God gives your physician the wisdom and knowledge to assist in your care, and there is nothing to be ashamed of if you need assistance from your doctor.

23

MOTHER'S PAIN

On November 16, 2011, mom took a fall at the top of an escalator inside Penn Station. Mom, Dosie, and one of mom's male adjutants were on their way to Virginia by train. After being in severe pain for almost two months and suffering with her left side, mom contacted my sister, and we contacted Steven. My sister made doctors' appointments immediately. Sunday morning January 15, 2012, mom called my sister, saying, "My legs hurt so badly I can hardly walk. I go up the stairs on my hands and knees. I come down the stairs by sliding on my back." Mom had explained a week earlier to us the fall she had taken was so hard that her shoe was flung from her left foot. When she fell onto the metal at the top of the escalator the male adjutant lost his balance, falling on top, further extending her chance for injuries. Mom told us she was hurting so bad after the hard fall that she could only lie there on the ground for a long while. We were told almost two months after the incident. I questioned the inner circle and mom as to what part the Pentecostal Christians do not understand.

I reiterated to Dosie and the inner circle once again, saying, "If it were your mom, I wouldn't have done that to you." I explained that it is a lot easier to allow us to assist and be involved in mom's health care rather than waiting for something to worsen like it had. The result of the fall in Penn Station placed mom into the Nyack Hospital on January 18, 2012. This was the start of mom's downward spiral. The inner circle and mom purposely maintained us running behind mom's health care until things with her health became unmanageable for them all. Dosie and the inner circle was seemingly treating mom's health as if it were some type of competition between the church and her children. Dosie and the inner circle's behaviors were very disturbing. I was left numb and confounded by the inner circle's lack of caring with their incensed attitudes toward their pastor's well-being and her family. When I questioned some of the inner circle, they made claim that they called me but did not get an answer. I just shook my head from side to side.

On January 18, 2012, mom called me around 5:00 p.m. complaining about the pain she felt in her legs and back.

Afterward I learned that mom had called my sister eight times or more during the day complaining of severe pain in her back and legs. Pam was away running arbitration meetings at the time. Mom began telling me how she wanted Dosie to bring her to ICM. ICM was a facility that was located in West Nyack, New York, that is recommended by some doctors for extensive outpatient physical therapy. I told her I would meet her there. When I arrived, they were doing acupuncture on her legs. I had never seen her in such pain. Tears began to swell up in my eyes. I asked the ICM technician to stop the treatment and call 911 for EMT services immediately. The Nanuet EMTs arrived within five minutes of the call. When I arrived at the hospital, no one from the Tabernacle Church was there. Mom asked me for two days where was everybody. My sister, brother, and I stayed around the clock assisting mom by turning her in different positions as she requested, trying to find some comfort for her pain. We would get mom to the potty or bring the potty to her. We washed her and looked after her care every day.

Melvin showed up on the second evening of mom's hospital stay. He appeared to be too sickly with noticeable weight loss and some type of sores on his arms and face. He told me that he was infected with some type of microorganisms in his bloodstream, which were similar to parasites from drinking water. Melvin held some type of electronic devise to his head, telling me that it was used to rid his body of these metallic microorganisms that had invaded his body and were everywhere inside of him. He told me that it was an act of the government trying to extract information from him. My brother in a quizzical voice said, "Why don't they just ask you for the information they are seeking." I was not quite sure if Melvin was delusional or if any part of his story was based on fact. At any point we had our hands filled with mom's situation and did not have time to follow up on Melvin's bizarre antics and stories. When I had a moment, I framed back to reflect on perhaps Melvin might be covering up some type of illness.

Finally late on Thursday Reverend Helen arrived and stayed for about twenty minutes or so. The doctors struggled with how to best relieve her pain and discomfort. The doctors explained that the problem is not a pathology problem that could be fixed easily. I thought, perhaps if I had known earlier, I could have gotten ahead of this with mom. This could have been avoided if the leadership regime had used better judgment. What happened to our mother's health should not have happened with this level of pain in this day and time. Dosie was supposed to be looking out for mom's well-being. I was at a complete loss by their behaviors. I found out the inner circle and some of the congregants expressed strongly they did not know my mother had fallen. They said, "Dosie kept it a secret from us that Pastor had fallen." My uncle Charlie, who is not a member of mom's church organization, said to me, "You can't blame that girl Dosie and those people. Your mother should have called you all herself." Dosie and mom have had an unusually close relationship for a pastor to a parishioner, seeming to be unnatural. Dosie and mother's bond appeared to be stronger than that of her inner circle.

The events that surrounded our mother's discharge from the hospital were like this: On January 23, 2012, mom's doctor spoke with me, telling me that mom was insistent that she felt better and wanted to be discharged. Mom was insistent that she was going home. Mom said to the inner circle group, "I want to go home." Dosie wrote a letter to the doctors and the inner circle in support of mom's hospital release. The letter was subsequent to Dosie staying the night with mom. Despite my encouragement and strong stance with mom, she would not stay in the hospital. I explained to the church leadership regime, Dosie, and

Reverend Helen that I was against mom leaving the hospital and did not condone her discharge to go home. Mom still needed professional care and rehabilitation as an inpatient at the Helen Hayes hospital. Dosie said she would take care of mom's health and arrange for mom's members to be at the house around the clock. I said at this point, "Please use your best judgment if you need to call me for any reason or no reason when it comes to my mom's health and wellness."

At this point mom sitting on the bed made an announcement to everyone by waving her hands into the air, as if she was waving a lantern in the darkness of night. Mom announced in her hospital room in a stark, unharmonious voice as if she was in the pulpit, "They can't call you if I don't release them to call you!" Mom had taken complete control over her parishioners' lives—wielding absolute power, control, and authority. They were merely acting as programmed robots. Mom and her church leadership regime moved the goal post further away from any understanding of their behavior, leaving me stunned and embarrassed. I framed back to July 2011 when Minister Lesley danced me around on the phone, and finally saying, "Mom never told me not to call you." Mom cleared up the confusion from the past as I got a quick dose of reality. Some preachers and Christians have become very comfortable and skillful at spinning facts and truths into falsehoods when directed by their leadership. The Tabernacle Church leadership acts and behaves without any parameters to being responsible to any form of moral standard to their congregants. Be that as it may. It is what it is.

The nursing and care team came to mom's hospital room with meticulous instruction as to how to care for mom. It was overwhelming if you were going to be involved with mom's direct care. Dosie was nowhere around. I stopped the registered nurse who was the program manager of patient and community education. I asked everyone, "Where's Dosie?" The nurses asked, "Who is going to be with mom at home?" They all responded and said, "Dosie." The RN said absolutely she had to be there. I asked the nurse if we could hold up until Dosie arrived. The nurse responded positively with, "Sure, that is no problem." I called Dosie on her cell phone and asked where she was. Dosie responded with, "At the house," meaning at my mother's house. I explained to her that mom was going to need particular care when she was discharged from the hospital and she needed to come down and hear what the regiment of care and wellness was going to involve. Dosie arrived in about thirty minutes, looking angered at my interrupting whatever she was doing at the house.

Dosie became more angry when I asked her to sign a release form for mom's pocketbook. I told them all I didn't want to hear a month from now that something was missing or I removed money or anything from mom's bag. Dosie refused to sign the form, so I wrote in her signature space these words "Refused to sign." I had Reverend Helen witness and Steven sign in the alternate space on the form. Earlier I had written about how Dosie influenced mom to make a report to the Stony Point Police Department that I stole $12,000 in saving bonds that belonged to my nephews. Once again I was reminded of the passage of scripture "Do not accuse anyone for no reason—when they have done you no harm" (Proverbs 3:30).

Mom started saying while in the hospital bed, "You have never taken anything from me, and I have always trusted my children." After this I started to assist Dosie in gathering mom's belongings for her to take home. Suddenly I noticed she disappeared. I asked Minister Lesley if he had seen Dosie. He responded by saying, "Dosie said her Acura and mom's Mercedes was too low to the ground for mom to get into." I called Dosie several times on her cell phone. She did not return my call or respond to my voice messages. I left the fourth floor with mom sitting in the wheelchair in Minister Lesley's care. Before I left, I asked Lesley if he could bring mom home. Lesley responded with, "I have to go pick up the baby, and my truck is too high for mom to get in." Mariah followed Lesley's excuse, saying in a servile voice, "I would drive Pastor except I don't have my truck. I have the car."

I turned away, leaving Mariah in the room, gathering all the stuff to be carried home—mom's clothing, flowers, and personal effects, etc. As I departed quickly to catch up to Dosie, I told Lesley and mom, "I am going to go look for Dosie." Shortly after I reached the downstairs visitor entrance, Lesley called me, saying, "Dosie is on the New York State Thruway." I said to Minister Lesley, "Tell her to come back here!"

Outside of the hospital waiting room I saw Bonnie, who was one of mom's faithful members, headed to her car. She was at the hospital because her sister Elaina had outpatient surgery. I explained to Bonnie that Dosie left the hospital and was on her way to mom's house without mom. I said to Bonnie, "Dosie left all the flowers, mom's clothes, personal effects, and mom sitting in the hallway with Minister Lesley." Bonnie chuckled and then told me that they all were sick of Dosie. Bonnie said, "Mom can go in the car with me and Elaina being that my car is right here at the front door." As I drove from the parking lot in search of Dosie who was holding the key to the house, Steven was placing the walker the hospital had given mom into the trunk of Bonnie's car with other items. Steven called me, saying, "Mom was screaming all I had asked James to do was to drive me home and he couldn't do that!" Steven said he told Mom, "You never asked James to drive you home. Plus James does not condone you leaving the hospital in this condition. You heard James when he came into the room. He told you and everybody he was against you leaving the hospital in your present condition, and he was not going to be a part of it while they all stood there and looked at him, including you."

I called mom later, and she said that I was supposed to drive her home. I told her no, no, no, saying, "Dosie left the hospital and did not communicate with me or anyone else." I told mother that it was unacceptable for her to do that, period. So I went to look for her. Besides she had all your personal belongings. Mom tried to convince me that Dosie was right! Mom said that Dosie carried things down to the car. I said to mom, "No, she took nothing, nor did she have anything in her hands." Mom defended Dosie by saying, "I told Dosie to go ahead." I said to mom, "Dosie did not communicate that to me, and I was right there in the bathroom pouring water from one of the vase of flowers that I was going to carry downstairs to assist her. When I asked where Dosie is, Lesley said 'She went into the elevator.' Minister Lesley then said, 'I think she left.' I responded by saying, 'What!'"

After mom's seeing my reaction, mom says, "I sent her ahead." And I say, "For what? You are there in the hallway, not at the house." Mom then stumbled around with some word games and said to me, "She is my parishioner, and she is following my orders. You have nothing to do with my parishioners when I give them orders." I then said, "Why did you send her to the house when you are here in the hallway?" Mom said, "All that don't matter. I sent her where I wanted her to go." I replied, "It may not matter to you, but it matters to me because it is affecting how we were going to get you home." Mom responded with, "Every time I get sick, you cause a ruckus." My reply to mom's was, "Mom, stop right there. I was not the one to not communicate. I was not the one to leave you sitting in the hallway. You are not being honest with your statement."

Mom continued to protect Dosie. With mother's encouragement, Dosie left the hospital being angry over the pocketbook release form. I was not going to allow them to say the son took the mother from the hospital. I was not going to abet and abate their uncaring actions and behaviors. It was apparent that the leadership regime told mother to be sure that I was the one to take her from the hospital. This all after my announcing that they could fall into negligence if this did not work out. It was obvious that if anything were to happen to our mother, they were in position to say the oldest son removed her from the hospital. When mother started spinning the hospital story with the confusion over my driving her home, it created attention. Mother's bizarre story brought a woman forward who I consider to be reliable.

Adding misery to pain, she told me, "Dosie did not want to drive your mom for this reason." The person began to tell me that Dosie's car was being paid for by a man named Everret. She continued by telling me that Everret is married and his wife had just learned recently of her husband paying for Dosie's white Acura. The informant told me, "Everett's wife could appear at any time to confront Dosie over this car business." All I could do once again was to shake my head from side to side.

The way that I could best describe mom's behavior is it is like dyslexia. However, reading was not mother's problem. Mom's handicap dealt with her family values operating in reverse. Mom would spin yarn with the result of people coming to me saying, "You have the best mother in the world. I wish she was my mother." By mother being a self-proclaimed woman of God and pastor added creditability to her bizarre, delusional volume of stories.

At this point mom and Dosie had the congregants coming into the house 24/7 to care for mom. I felt very strongly that mom needed to be at Helen Hayes rehabilitation facility before going home. Mom said, "God is going to give her a miracle as the prednisone wears off." I checked on mom's health and well-being daily. She was curt and vague, most times rude. She is my mom and I intend to ask her every day how she is doing and if she needs me to do anything for her. Mom in her affliction stumbled around searching for blame to tarnish her family in the judgment of her congregants and associates. This was unmistakably unnatural behavior to me, my sister, and brother. When I called home to check on mom, the home phone would ring and ring. Mom's cell phone would go to her voice mail. The inner circle of ministers would not answer or return my calls as well. E-mails and text messages also went unanswered. I was not sure what I should do beyond this point, if anything.

Mom and the inner circle six started the rumor mill circulation that her children wanted to see her dead. Mom said I tried to kill her in the hospital by giving her an overdose injection of morphine. I thought to myself, *If I were trying to kill her, why would she want to get into a car with me?* My heart led me to say mom's suffering was brought on by vain worship. Mom's deliverance and freedom from her torment and physical pain are through God's grace principles and respecting the fabric of family values. Mom still, after the years gone by, harbors the notion that I want to take over her church. The church leadership regime continues to reinforce this attitude with mom. It is sad, actually pathetic, and cruel on the behalf of her inner circle to behave in this manner.

I often thought, *What are mom and the inner circle covering up with finger-pointing and defiance to any reasonability?* Governments, businesses, corporations, and people have used brands of distraction for years to lure people's attention away from what is really going on by pointing away from the real conditions. There is no back door for mom's church to egress from these circumstances. Mother has become accustomed to the showboating and showcasing. Not only my mother but also any pastor attempting to break the union and brand of vain worship will present an immense challenge to change their behavior.

The art of understanding is what you cannot see, not so much what you see on the surface with the naked eye. Real understanding comes when you listen with your inner ear. Clarity comes to focus when you are able to truly see another's heart. Whether a person has good or evil in their heart, you can gain the skill and savvy to listen with an inner ear, getting the understanding of what is really being said. Most of us don't say what we mean. Many forms of communications and messages are mixed with perceptions, generalizations, and sound bites. Perception is nine-tenths reality.

On Wednesday, February 1, my brother spoke with mom. He wanted to check on her condition and pain level. The conversation turned into mom telling him, along with others, that I wanted to see her dead. Mother tells people her children want to see her dead when she falls ill and lands into the hospital. Mom and I disagreed with her leaving the hospital and not pursuing physical therapy as one of the first steps to her recovery as the doctor had requested.

At this point, I recapped the events of mother's hospital visit with Steven to ensure we were all on the same page. Far too often our family has been left in a position of justification to fabricated stories where we had no voice to redress these types of allegations. Mom made a huge deal about me going to find Dosie who had mom's personals and all her keys. Minister Lesley told me that Dosie said "My car and mom's Mercedes is too low for mom to get in" as she headed into the elevator, which made no sense to me. Dosie drove a four-door Acura, which was larger than my vehicle. Dosie dropped everything, leaving the hospital with mom in a wheelchair sitting in the hospital hallway. I called Dosie twice. She never responded to my call or voice messages. Mom covered up for Dosie by telling Steven that she could send her parishioner wherever she wanted. Mom said, "Dosie or no one else has to communicate to James. *He ain't nobody!*" Steven said, "Mom, there are two thoughts going on here. (1) Dosie is telling Minister Lesley she cannot take you home because her car was too low. (2) You say you sent her away. Which is it?"

Mom's flawed family values intensified with the side effects of all the medication she was taking. It appeared to underscore her unreasonableness. Tears welted in my eyes as I felt mom was losing ground by her absolute position in making her family her adversary. In the hours of her most physical and severe pain, she pointed a condemning finger to her children being the crisis in her life and church. Her inner circle fell way short of providing a healthy balance of attention to our mom. I have often admittedly felt brokenhearted and painfully ashamed of the estranged relationship that exists between mom and me. The inner circle led congregants to believe that mom had to be protected from her children and grandchildren. Mom furthered her actions by infusing more ill-fated stories telling folks I tried to kill her in the hospital. She publicly announced that her children wanted to see her dead.

The inner circle and mom fabricated to her associates and congregants her family had abandoned her during her illness. No one in the Tabernacle Church organization took the courage to stand up for family morals or our family. The truth for our family, we are immobilized; we can't help our mother escape the bewitching and cannot eradicate her from the destruction of vain worship. It is like treading on water looking for a bottom, and there isn't one. I believe that God intended for people to have a family.

Our family remains diligent under prayer with the cover of faith and wishful thoughts for a positive turnaround. I don't blame mother for gleaning attention. It's the way she has gone about it that is troublesome. Hurting people, diminishing family values, the profanation of God's grace principles are not the way to go about life for any reason. For a mother wanting to turn her children over to hands that do not have the best interest for her family is incomparable behavior. Mom often made this statement after privately held family discussions: "I will have to go tell the people about this." Mom would twist family conversations and discussions into her being victimized by her children. My heart aches for our mother. Where is the accountability of intentional acts of a church leadership regime to fall, and onto whose shoulders?

In August 2014, mother called my sister to tell her she can no longer withstand the pain she was enduring. She told my sister she had to find some type of relief and demanded her doctor to do surgery or anything necessary for her to find some respite. The doctor put things on pause until he could stabilize mother's multiple health problems. Mom's doctor had explained to me two years ago that there was no pathology to fixing her problem. However, we remained faithful, hopeful, and prayerful for mother's mind and health to be made anew. Many prophecies such as what Bishop Shorts and Brown forecasted on July 18, 2013, have gone forth. These forecasts claimed that God said mom's body would be healed, period. I noticed they only prayed for her physiology and not for the restoration of her mind and body as a whole person. Mother was sanctioned by bishops, preachers, ministers, evangelist, and other church corporate leaders to make her family her number one enemy. This is abusive of "absolute faith and absolute power." Controlled by religious elitism and money! Mother usually point an accusing finger to people faced with afflictions as doing something against her and were being punished by God for their actions. Mom, now with her illness, says it's an attack of the enemy.

This has become a difficult situation for our family to come out of, right side up. No matter the circumstances we face or how unreceptive the condition may be, and you've done all you can, the Word of God says speak to your situation. After you speak to your circumstance, follow through with God's process: believe and be grounded by faith. Accept and respect the outcome and purpose of what God delivers. My God can do anything—anything! He can pick you up, dust you off, and put you back together. He is shelter in and out of storms. I am so grateful!

24

YOU ARE A WINNER

WE ALL WANT TO BE a winner. That is one of the reasons you might have chosen to place your life and heart into God's hands. Christlike grace in your everyday life is what makes you a winner. There are times when God will use injury or the storms in our lives to draw us closer to him. Winners come away from battles and competitions with mental, spiritual, and physical conditions altered after being the victor. The internal and physical evidence of a battle shows scarring, broken bones, or bruises. Painful injuries, internal or external, sometimes manifest and identify one as a victor, even though the external conditions look like a loss. As Christ hung on the cross, it looked like a defeat. Christ was a winner. He had the markings of a winner—nailed, scarred hands, blood streaming down from his sides. His forehead had the imprint of the thorns that he was crowned with. We understand the visible and spiritual signs of Christ being an embattled winner for our sake.

The Bible story of Joseph gives an example of a winner. Joseph's life was filled with evil actions that he had no control over. His brother, jealous of their father's favor toward Joseph, faked his death and sold him into slavery. The Midianites sold Joseph in Egypt to Potiphar, one of Pharaoh's officials, the captain of the guard (Genesis 37:35–36 NIV). Later, Joseph was falsely accused by Potiphar's wife of rape and thrown into prison. Joseph had much to be angry about, but he didn't give into bitterness. Instead, he let God turn his circumstances into something great. Joseph reacted and answered each new challenge in his life by not giving into the temptation of despair and kept moving forward.

For many of us, we would sooner withdraw than seek to find greater purpose in our place. We victimize ourselves and consider ourselves deserving of the bitterness we harbor, all the while ignoring how the bitterness is only hurting us and making matters worse. We turn our entire situation inward and grow more angry with each passing day, and then we convince ourselves that no one could possibly understand and that no one is worthy of identifying with the pain we have felt. Granted, the pain was real and the hurt very personal, but the bottom line is that we have a choice as to what that pain and hurt becomes. It can either be evil that remains evil, or it can be turned around by God to bring something that is good.

There is so much in this world meant for evil, and there is so much we will suffer as a result of that evil. But there is a God who is far greater, and there is a potential for good to be brought out from all things. We do not have to allow evil to hurt us to the point of permanently robbing our joy. We do not have to allow evil to imprison us in an eternal withdrawal and disillusionment. There is a victory that can come out of the worst circumstances and a joy that can radiate from a wounded heart. All because God can take what some mean for evil and use it to accomplish greater things.

One aspect of the Bible is how it exposes the failings of its heroes. For example, take Moses, David, and Paul, if the Bible were a straight hagiography of these "heroes of the faith," we would read only of their mighty accomplishments, and we wouldn't find any mention of their failings. The Bible writings seemed to not be interested in whitewashing the lives and actions of great heroes. Their flaws are described alongside their virtues. And it's often the case that their failings teach us just as much or more about living in faith than do their mighty deeds.

A moment of reflection: Have you ever feared losing your job where you would put your integrity at risk? Have you ever feared being ridiculed or misunderstood? Would you neglect your reputation by not sharing the truth if it meant placing someone's eternity at risk?

If you've ever felt intimidation or fear, then be assured that only one thing will conquer your fears: tenacious faith in God—in His presence, His protection, His power, His promises. Just remember, God is bigger than your biggest fear! Fear is nothing more than the evidence of what appears to be real.

Imagine that a future biographer is describing your life and accomplishments. What flaws might they point out? Are you allowing that flaw to define your life and relationship to God, or are you asking God to give your victory over it? God is a fortress, which we can find protection from life's storms. God's Word and wisdom protects us from spiritual harm. Your hurt, your shame, your broken heart, your broken spirit—you don't have to live with it or hide it from yourself to survive. You can turn your injuries, those bruises and broken hearts, into victory.

In one of my darkest moment, I had reinforcement that "He is light without a source, without a shadow." No one is exempt from encumbrances from this life, or the battles of competitions. Injuries and scars can be evident to your being a winner!

25

GET READY, GET READY

ARE CHURCHES REALLY GETTING READY for the end of the world? What are church corporations doing to prepare for the end of time? Do preachers, priest, ministers, and evangelist really believe in what the Bible says based on their behaviors and actions? Or are they just fooling some of the people some of the time?

May 20, 2011, pastor and radio host Harold Camping's predicted that the world would end on May 21, 2011, at 6:00 p.m. For years, eighty-nine-year-old Harold Camping has stood firm on the date the world would end. Camping reassured the world that on May 21, 2011, is when the rapture would take place. For those left behind, there would have been earthquakes followed by months of mayhem and destruction until October 21 when the world would end.

After Camping's prediction did not come true, Camping reset the date to October 21, 2011. October 21, 2011, was yet another false alarm by Camping. How many more alerts and prophecies have come and passed? After so much kudu, hype, and national news coverage about Camping and others predictions, I was prompted to ask this question, How many more alerts and prophecies have come and past?

How does one get ready for the world to end? What do you do in preparation for this event? I spoke with a friend who took a telephone call from a coworker who was calling out of work May 20 through May 22, 2011. My thought was, *Why call out of work if you believe the world is going to end? It won't matter.*

On May 20, 2011, *Time* in partnership with CNN put together a list of end-of-world prophecies. Here are some of the prophecies:

Harold Camping, 1994
By Claire Suddath

Harold Camping's prediction that the world will end Saturday, May 21, 2011, is not his first such prediction. In 1992, the evangelist published a book called 1994? Which proclaimed that sometime in mid-September 1994, Christ would return and the world would end? Camping based his calculations on numbers and dates found in the Bible and, at the time, said that he was "99.9% certain" that his math was correct. But the world did not end in 1994. Nor did it end on March 31, 1995—another date Camping provided when September 1994 passed without incident. "I'm like the boy who cried wolf again and again and the wolf didn't come," Camping told the San Francisco Chronicle in 1995. "This doesn't bother me in the slightest."

The Millerites
By Kayla Webley

William Miller is perhaps the most famous false prophet in history. In the 1840s he began to preach about the world's end, saying Jesus Christ would return for the long-awaited Second Coming and that Earth would be engulfed in fire sometime between March 21, 1843, and March 21, 1844. He circulated his message in public gatherings and by using the technologies of the day—posters, printed newsletters and charts. Moved by those messages, as many as 100,000 "Millerites" sold their belongings between 1840 and 1844 and took to the mountains to wait for the end. When that end didn't come, Miller changed the date to Oct. 22. When Oct. 23 rolled around, his loyal followers explained it away yet again and went on to form the Seventh-day Adventist movement.

Just before sunset on Feb. 28, 1963, residents of northwestern Arizona watched what the Arizona Republic called a "strikingly beautiful and mysterious cloud" glide across the desert. That same day, Pentecostal Pastor William Branham—who founded the post–World War II faith-healing movement—climbed Sunset Mountain and claimed he met with seven angels who revealed to him the meaning of the seven seals from the Book of Revelation. Days later, Branham returned to his congregation at the Branham Tabernacle in Jeffersonville, Ind. He preached seven sermons in seven nights, explaining the meaning of the seals and the seven visions he had received, leading him to predict that Jesus would return to Earth in 1977. He did not live to see the day. In December 1965, as Branham was driving with his family in Texas, a drunk driver smashed into his car. Branham died six days later, on Christmas Eve.

The Anabaptists of Munster
By Ishaan Tharoor

In the tumultuous years that followed the Protestant Reformation, myriad radical sects emerged, preaching an apocalyptic, millenarianist creed that perturbed even theological dissidents like Martin Luther. The Anabaptists derived their name from the Latin for "one who baptizes over again" and rejected most forms of political organization and social hierarchy in favor of an idealized theocratic commonwealth. In the 1530s, riding on a crest of peasant revolts, a clutch of Anabaptists assumed control of the German town of Munster and hailed it as a New Jerusalem awaiting the return of Christ.

But the situation in Munster was far from the ideal Christian commonwealth. Jan Bockelson, a tailor from the Dutch city of Leiden, declared himself the "Messiah of the last days," took multiple wives, issued coins that prophesied the coming apocalypse and in general made life hell for everyone in the city (except for a few fellow proselytizers who lived lavishly—and, according to some accounts, in a great state of debauch). The Anabaptists' hold over Munster ended in a bloody siege in 1535. Bockelson's genitals reportedly were nailed to the city's gates.

Late Great Planet Earth and Other Prophecy Books
By Kayla Webley

If you follow Hal Lindsey, you've probably changed the "end of the world" date in your calendar several times. His Late Great Planet Earth, which was the best-selling nonfiction book of the 1970s, predicted that the world would end sometime before Dec. 31, 1988. He cited a host of world events—nuclear war, the communist threat and the restoration of Israel—as reasons the end times were upon mankind. His later books, though less specific, suggested that believers not plan on being on Earth past the 1980s—then the 1990s and, of course, the 2000s. But Lindsey did more than just wrongly predict the end of days; he popularized a genre of prophecy books.

Adding stock to Lindsey's original claim, Edgar Whisenant published a book in 1988 called 88 Reasons Why the Rapture Will Be in 1988, which sold some 4.5 million copies. Whisenant once famously said, "Only if the Bible is in error am I wrong." When 1989 rolled around, a discredited Whisenant published another book, saying the Rapture would occur that year instead. It did not sell as well, nor did later titles that predicted the world would end in 1993 and again in 1994. The genre's most popular tales are in the Left Behind series, written by Tim LaHaye and Jerry Jenkins, which, though they do not predict an end date, provide a vivid fictional account of how Earth's final days could go. The 16 novels have sold more than 63 million copies worldwide.

Y2K
By Frances Romero

It was the day that was supposed to finally prove what Luddites and other tech haters had been saying for so long: computers—not sin or religious prophecy come true—will bring us down. For months before the stroke of midnight on Jan. 1, 2000, analysts speculated that entire computer networks would crash; causing widespread dysfunction for a global population that had become irreversibly dependent on computers to hold, disseminate and analyze its most vital pieces of information. The problem was that many computers had been programmed to record dates using only the last two digits of every year, meaning that the year 2000 would register as the year 1900, totally screwing with the collective computerized mind. But it just wasn't so. Aside from a few scattered power failures in various countries, problems in data-transmission systems at some of Japan's nuclear plants (which did not affect their safety) and a temporary interruption in receipt of data from the U.S.'s network of intelligence satellites, the New Year arrived with nothing more than the expected hangover.

The Branch Davidians
By Frances Romero

David Koresh led his Branch Davidian sect, an unsanctioned offshoot of the Seventh-day Adventist Church, to its doom in a compound near Waco, Texas, in 1993. How did he do that? He convinced his followers that he was Christ and that they should hole up at what was called the Mount Carmel Center to prepare for the end of the world. Their ideas were based on the beliefs of an earlier Adventist splinter group.

When authorities learned that the Branch Davidians were allegedly holding a trove of weapons on the site and that there were possibly instances of abuse of women and children, the Bureau of Alcohol, Tobacco, Firearms and Explosives executed a search on the compound in February 1993. The Davidians fought back; four agents were killed as well as six members of the sect. Koresh persuaded his followers to remain at Mount Carmel and refuse to surrender. For 50 days, a tense standoff ensued. On April 19, the FBI stormed the compound, a fire erupted (the source of which is still debated), and dozens of Davidians, including Koresh, died in the building.

Jehovah's Witnesses
By Frances Romero

The onset of World War I freaked a lot of people out. But it was especially trippy for the Zion's Watch Tower Tract Society, a group that's now called

Jehovah's Witnesses. The society's founder, Charles Taze Russell, had previously predicted Christ's invisible return in 1874, followed by anticipation of his Second Coming in 1914. When WW I broke out that year, Russell interpreted it as a sign of Armageddon and the upcoming end of days or, as he called it, the end of "Gentile times." History proved otherwise.

The Great London Fire of 1666
By Nate Rawlings

In the Christian tradition, the number 666 is described as the "mark of the beast" in the Bible's Book of Revelation. So it was no surprise that Europeans worried as the year 1666 approached. It didn't help that the year before; a plague had wiped out about 100,000 people, a fifth of London's population, leading many to predict the end of times. Then on Sept. 2, 1666, a fire broke out in a bakery on London's Pudding Lane. The fire spread and over three days burned more than 13,000 buildings and destroyed tens of thousands of homes. But in the end, fewer than 10 people perished in the blaze, which, while catastrophic, was not the end of the world. This is what the Associated Press reported on May 21, 2011, after the disappointment by many when the end of time did not come as predicted by Harold Camping. What do we make of this?

Christian Movement Preparing for End of Days
By Garance Burke

Some shut themselves inside to pray for mercy as they waited for the world's end. Others met for tearful last lunches with their children, and prepared to leave behind homes and pets as they were swept up to heaven. And across the globe, followers of a California preacher's long-publicized message that Judgment Day would arrive Saturday turned to the Bible, the book they believe predicts the beginning of Earth's destruction on May 21. The doomsday message has been sent far and wide via broadcasts and web sites by Harold Camping, an 89-year-old retired civil engineer who has built a multi-million-dollar nonprofit ministry based on his apocalyptic prediction...

After spending months traveling the country to put up Judgment Day billboards and hand out Bible tracts, Camping follower Michael Garcia planned to spend Friday evening with his family at home in Alameda, near the Christian media empire's Oakland headquarters. They believe it will likely start as it becomes 6 p.m. in the world's various time zones." We know the end will begin in New Zealand and will follow the sun and roll on from there," said Garcia, a 39-year-old father of six. "That's why God raised up all the technology and the satellites so everyone can see it happen at the same time."

The Internet was alive with reaction in the hours past 6 p.m. Saturday in New Zealand. "Harold Camping's 21st May Doomsday prediction fails; No earthquake in New Zealand," read one posting on Twitter. "If this whole end-of-the-world thingy is still going on...it's already past 6.00 in New Zealand and the world hasn't ended," said another.

Camping's radio stations, TV channels, satellite broadcasts and website are controlled from a humble building on the road to the Oakland International Airport, sandwiched between an auto shop and a palm reader. Family Radio International's message has been broadcast in 61 languages. Camping, however, will be awaiting Jesus Christ's return for the second time. He said his earlier apocalyptic prediction in 1994 didn't come true because of a mathematical error. "I'm not embarrassed about it. It was just the fact that it was premature," he told The Associated Press last month. But this time, he said, "there is… no possibility that it will not happen."

Skeptics are planning Rapture-themed parties to celebrate what hosts expect will be the failure of the world to come to an end. Bars and restaurants from Melbourne, Australia to the Florida Keys advertised bashes. In Oakland, atheists planned a gathering at a local Masonic temple to include group discussions on "The Great Success of Past Apocalypses," followed by dinner and music.

Camping and his followers believe the beginning of the end will come on May 21, exactly 7,000 years since the flood in the biblical story of Noah's Ark. Some 200 million people will be saved, Camping preaches, and those left behind will die in earthquakes, plagues, and other calamities until Earth is consumed by a fireball on October 21. In the Philippines, a big billboard of Family Radio ministry in Manila warned of Judgment Day. Earlier this month, group members there distributed leaflets to motorists and carried placards warning of the end of the world.

Christian leaders from across the spectrum have widely dismissed the prophecy, but one local church is concerned that Camping's followers could slip into a deep depression come Sunday. Pastor Jacob Denys of Milpitas-based Calvary Bible Church plans to wait outside the nonprofit's headquarters on Saturday afternoon, hoping to counsel believers who may be disillusioned if the Rapture does not occur. "The cold, hard reality is going to hit them that they did this, and it was false and they basically emptied out everything to follow a false teacher," he said. "We're not all about doom and gloom. Our message is a message of salvation and of hope."

On Friday afternoon, a small group of eccentrics, gawkers and media opportunists convened outside Family Radio's closed office building. A sign posted on the front door said "SORRY WE MISSED YOU!" As May 21 drew nearer, followers say donations grew, allowing Family Radio to spend millions of dollars on more than 5,000 billboards and 20 RVs plastered with the doomsday message. In 2009, the nonprofit reported in IRS filings that it received $18.3 million in donations, and had assets of more than $104 million, including $34 million in stocks or other publicly traded securities.

Marie Exley, who helped put up apocalypse-themed billboards in Israel, Jordan, Lebanon and Iraq, said the money helped the nonprofit save as many souls as possible. She said she and her husband, mother and brother planned to stay glued to the television Friday night in Bozeman, Montana for news of an earthquake in New Zealand.

Camping recommended this week that followers surround themselves by their loved ones and not meet publicly, Exley said.

"It's an emotional time and we're kind of nervous and scared about how things will pan out as to who will be here and who will go to heaven," she said. "I'll probably be scared in the fog of it, and crying, because we don't know who is saved and who is not."

Some people wanted to make sure their pets receive good treatment, no matter what happens. Sharon Moss, who founded AfterTheRapturePetCare. com to provide post-apocalypse animal care, said a new wave of customers has paid $10 to sign up in the last few weeks. A lot of people have said you should be out there saving souls not saving pets but my heart says "why can't you do both?" said Moss, who identifies herself as Protestant.

May 21ˢᵗ came and went, without the prediction and prophecy being fulfilled. This is not the first or the last of prophecies that I have seen not come to fruition. Who will be the next person or group to make the announcement as to when the rapture will take place? I learned from my mom at an early age, based on the biblical beliefs and scripture: "The Day and Hour Unknown But about that day or hour no one knows, not even the angels in heaven, nor the Son, but only the Father" Matthew 24:35–37 (NIV).

26

GOD'S GRACE PRINCIPLES

Growing into adolescent, I witnessed preachers blaring from pulpits with ear-piercing warnings that "Jesus is coming back at any moment." This all before the preacher made a convincing and appealing altar call for sinners and backsliders, followed up with, "Will you be ready when he comes?" What I heard then, I still hear today in a less significant form. Preachers today have shifted more attention toward prophecies of material prosperity. You see the Bible is a textbook of ontology and metaphysics. It perceives all things in the connection to the human soul. For example, the word *bread* is not merely physical food. It has a broader interpretation than the literal sense of food. Bread inferences all things that man requires such as clothing, shelter, money, education, and so forth. Above all it stands for spiritual things such as spiritual perception, spiritual understanding, spiritual realization. "Give us this day our daily bread. I am the bread of life."

Another example is the word prosperity. When we hear and think of prosperity, we usually think of material comfort, success, and wealth on the planet—sort of, who has the most money, gadgets, and toys win. In the scriptural sense *prosperity* and *prosper* signify a great deal more than the acquirement of material possessions. They mean success in prayer. From the point of view of the soul, success in prayer is the only kind of prosperity worth having. A certain quantity of material goods is essential on this planet, of course, but material wealth is the least important thing in life, and this the Bible implies by giving the word *prosperous* its true meaning. Wealth is the least important thing.

The Tabernacle leadership preserves the congregants on high alert that Jesus could crack the sky at any moment. However, the leadership regime handles situations so vicariously, having little to no sensitivity to others. Some church leadership regimes direct congregants to where and whom they should worship, leaving congregants with ideological judgment of others. Just going to church does not make you a Christian any more than standing in your garage makes you a car. Every saint has a past. Every sinner has a future!

Every church reserves the right to feel they have the greatest minister on earth. I believe ministers should be encouraged and felt appreciated. However, there must be consideration and boundaries to unproductive worship. We hold a high regard for ministers. When ministers diligently pursue God's principles of grace, we cannot fully express the appreciation and gratitude that is often deserved. Living through my firsthand experiences, it is apparent that church corporations in America are in disrepair. So many churches have lost their moral sense of responsibility to self-governance. Who is to bear the blood on their hands of so many unsuspecting brokenhearted?

Remember to apply God's grace and His grace principles to yours and others' lives. When confusion enters your life, think of this: Confusion is good. It allows us to sort out and clear things up.

Even though mom preferred a few of her church followers over her family, and amid the dismal dealing of mother's psychological disenchantments, the truth is, in the thick of things, mother will always be loved and will always hold the distinction of being our mom. Maybe someday, somewhere, someone will extend their hand to genuinely welcome an orphaned pastor's family to an environment that worships God and serves its congregants by teaching Gods principles of divine grace.

I and my family count it a blessing and are eternally grateful to have served and worshiped with so many. This book is written with heartfelt experiences to offer a sobering challenge to worshipers to be more informed. I have written to the honor of the church brokenhearted that had no voice in their church. I pray this venue will help in the healing process of mending broken hearts. If one word leads to one heart being changed or placing congregants into a greater capacity to earnestly serve others, then this book will have served a purpose.

The facts I brought forward have not challenged or changed the love and appreciation I have for our mom, family, other families, pastors, ministers, and church families. I was brought up in church. I know what can happen publicly and behind closed doors of a church organization and its leadership regimes. I pray and trust that my church experiences and story bring some understanding and comfort to the departed church brokenhearted.

I have been reflective, direct, and untiring in my writing to the churches' brokenhearted. My church experiences have matured my appreciation to look further than the frailties of life with the strength of a forgiving heart. Some of God's plans and understanding of the purpose of our lives are sometimes hard to accept. I admonish all to look to a higher power outside of man for strength. As I had written earlier, the Bible is filled with stories of redemption. Hurting people hurt people. Broken church relationships create broken people. I have learned through Christ to look beyond my church experiences and beyond the crosses we bear.

I leave these thoughts: One word frees us of all the weight and pain of life. That word is love. For one human being to love another, that is perhaps the most difficult of all our tasks, the ultimate, the last test and proof, the work for which all other work is but preparation. Lastly, wisdom of your heart is the love of God, and it is the greatest gift we can hope to share with others. Remember, there is life after church.

My daily meditation prayer:

> My Heavenly Father, I pray in the power of the Holy Spirit, I give you thanks for all things. I thank you for keeping me mindful of Your abounding grace. Father, I bind, rebuke, cast out, and bring to no effect all spirits of division, disunity, condemnation, envy, jealousy, slander, complaining, lying, false teaching,

poverty, and fear spirits. I bind and break all curses that have been spoken against me.

I pray for those who curse me and who spitefully use me. I ask for your forgiveness for negative thoughts or judgments I have made against others for no reason. I bind the power of negativity and render useless all thoughts not inspired by the Holy Spirit. I am Your child. I take authority over this day in Jesus's name. Let this day be prosperous for me and others as I walk in the love of Jesus Christ. Heavenly Father, I pray for Your Holy Spirit to guide me through the day bringing no harm upon anyone. I bind evil forces from my family, my mind, my body, my home, and finances. I confess that I am healed and whole. Today I will flourish and love. Whatsoever I set my hands to do shall prosper for God who is able to supply all of my needs.

I pray for the ministry You have for me. Anoint me for what You have called me to do on this day. I claim a hedge of protection around myself and my family. I pray that you will send Your angels to protect my home from intrusion and to protect our earthly belongings. Protect us from harmful demonic physical or mental attacks. I ask this prayer in the name of Jesus as I give your name the glory, the Son of the Living God. Amen.

Over the years there have been changes we've all gone through, harm that we experience and have given to others. Being thoughtless and cruel painfully hurts people. We can only hope and believe we are forgiven for any hurt that we were at fault. There is not anything more important than family. On behalf of me and my family, we value your prayers for us and other families. The Alston family leaves a legacy to implicate building family relations, responsible moral conduct, with accountability. Those closest to us should be the easiest to love rather than the easiest to hurt.

As of November 2013, mom asks for her family to rejoin her ministry and assist with the Tabernacle Church Incorporated. This presented an immense challenge to our family as we lean forward to a position of healing and reckoning. My brother without inquiry and with mom's coercing reversed himself and returned to manage the hair salon. In addition, Steven took on a position to be mother's advisor and spiritual consultant.

In March 2014, Steven advertised the salon as if it were a new business by launching its debut on Facebook. He posted on their Facebook page one outsized portrait of himself with a few less significant photos of mother with small groups of people. Steven, Tessy, and the inner circle church management took photo ops promoting the salon as if it were continually open; however, there were no hair stylists.

During this time my brother cozies up to Dosie, mother, and the inner circle group, reversing his position on publishing this book. Previously, after Steven submitted his written e-mail statements to me, I couldn't publish this book soon enough to his taste. I learned mother and Dosie destabilized Steven by offering him financial benefits to support their agendas. I don't blame him. Everyone has a price. The original contract the leadership agreed and signed off on with me remains active. Based on my history of experiences with the church leadership, I retain a position of vigilance. As of today the Faith Educational Center and hair salon remain out of use for going on fourteen years. Putting all things aside, my principled belief is simply God, family, and love.

Men are like sheep, effortlessly led to their demise by uncaring leadership regimes. Numerous parishioners feel vulnerable to their legitimate fears and easily neglect facing their responsibility to defend God's grace principles. They prefer to remain sightless to church dysfunctional conditions, so much so until it becomes painfully obvious to onlookers. It takes courage to handle adversity. Innumerable churches have been led into a quagmire of a conundrum by poor leadership. Church corporations splurge inconceivable amounts of money and resources into image management and damage control. We often view the pastor as someone who is not human; however, we must remember pastors are human and can hurt like anyone else. An inestimable number of preachers lead you to believe that what they say is Bible based when actually it's just a matter of personal predilection. Not all churches have abandoned the application of the gospel although a great number of ministries have gone off course. We pray for leaders to give consideration to God's grace principles and the quality of biblical values. I have digressed from evangelical culture and movements that church corporations have created. Although most of us work at keeping our life filled with positive interactions. Folks do have a tendency to scoop out the positive things from your life, replacing them with negatives. Donald O. Clifton, PhD, says, "It's important to note that we don't recommend ignoring negativity and weakness; *positivity must be grounded in reality.*"

I trust this genre is a voice for the silenced church brokenhearted. Perhaps each and every one of our church experiences has made for a better someone. There is always something tragic about disappointments and our fallen idols. The tragedy is, how could we have been so wrong? Never believe someone's light is brighter than your own. Ernest Hemingway once said, "In order to write about life first you must live it."

THAT WAS THEN, THIS IS NOW

Mom and I sat on the couch in the family room as we discussed her vision that God had bequeath her with for the ministry of St. John Deliverance Tabernacle Church Incorporated.

Nothing unusual was going on. It was a fair and calm evening on April 8, 2019 around 8:00 pm. Mom's parakeet, Peter was standing on top of his cage. Doing his usual performance by whistling.

Over Peter's whistling, Mom and I discussed church business; concerning the vision that God had placed in her heart. Alwhile having a small glass table in front of her with a tasty meal. We continued with the church business discussion while she enjoyed her steak from one of her favorite restaurants, Hogan's in Stony Point.

I made an inquiry to my Mother saying, "Mom…should you be eating that this late?" In her character, Mom looked over at me and said, "Would you like some?" We both gave each other a wide smile. After we were done with the church business, we bid each other a goodnight with a hug.

I was not prepared for what was about to happen. On April 9th I was in Orangeburg, New York. I received a frantic phone call that Mom was not well, and had fallen onto the floor in her bedroom. I was about twenty minutes away. I asked the person that was in the house with Mom to call 911.

I arrived about fifteen minutes later. The Emergency Medical Team was already there. They had Mom in the ambulance. I could see her on the stretcher. The EMT's were saying, "Stay with us Elizabeth…Stay with us…"

Mom was admitted into Good Samaritan hospital on April 9th in critical condition. It was one of the most difficult times of my life.

Mom was in and out of consciousness. I was sitting at the foot of her bed, when she became alert. Mom called out to me saying, "James come here…" I stood up and went to her bedside. With the I V tubes in her arms and monitoring wires; Mom reached out to me with open arms to hug me. As I hugged her she said, "I am so sorry." I responded and said, "Mom it's alright…it's alright…" I sat back down. Mom called me to her bedside two more times, saying the same words as before. I began to weep, unable to hold the tears back.

Mom had dispatched Steven with her blessings to the Philippines.

Mom sanctioned Steven to spearhead the outreach ministry. A vision God bestowed on her for St. John Deliverance Tabernacle Ministry.

Our Mother laid her cross down to transition from this life on April 16, 2019. Steven rushed back from the Philippines. Steven was able to see Mother before she departed this life…

During the grieving of our Mother's death, Tony Via and the defendants initiated their plan to take over St. John Deliverance Tabernacle Church, Incorporated.

Tony Via was the puppet master behind the actions of the defendants. Contiguous to our Mom's death Tony Via who titled himself the Pastor's Adjutant and driver. Tony had been at the church for a number of years.

Tony married Mischell Scott, who is the niece of Sarah Allen; Sarah Allen also having long tenure at the church.

Prior to our Mother's death, Sarah Allen and our Mom were not on the best of terms. Sarah had made plans to leave St. John Deliverance Tabernacle Church and relocate to North Carolina.

Unexpectedly, upon our Mother's death Sarah Allen decided to jump back and team up with Tony Via. The master plan by Via was to install Sarah as the Senior Pastor and Tony would take the roll of Executive Pastor. Then at some point Allen would pass the reins onto Tony Via and his family.

Self-appointed Senior Pastor Tony Via, Sarah Allen along with their defendants made a sober decision. That decision was to completely dissolve and remove Steven and myself from the ministry.

Via, Allen and defendants first order of their ill gotten plan was to vacate Steven and me from the church. They stop all verbal, electronic, written or otherwise. Our phone calls to Sarah Allen, Tony Via and their defendants were shrugged off. Our supposition was this can't be happening.

We were placed into a position without any other choice but to seek legal intervention.

The defendants' fickleness resulted in Steven and me placing our story into the media's hands. A local paper published our article which read as such:

Determined Brothers Fight to
Restore their Mother's Legacy

The hijacking and takeover of a Church
in Nyack has led to legal challenges

There is a great injustice being committed by parishioners who assemble at St. John Deliverance Tabernacle Church located at 35 Piermont Avenue in Nyack, New York. The Offences are: 1) Operating illegally 2) blocking the Alston family from continuing and fulfilling the vision and mission of the founding Pastor, their mother; which is to provide opportunities for expression of worship and community services that will enhance the lives of individuals.

Pastor Elizabeth Alston led this thriving Church for 53 years until her passing in 2019 when she suddenly took sick, was hospitalized and never recovered. Her two sons, James and Steven Alston have been working by her side since the inception of the Church. Both of her sons James and Steven held integral positions with the founder's intentions for them to remain in key positions to ensure the fulfillment of her mission.

The mission is not being fulfilled and the vision is being bastardized. Her vision entails building partnerships to offer educational opportunities, housing for the homeless as well as social services within the community and international services to those in need. However, this devious scheme to railroad her life's mission was initiated while she was incapacitated by falsifying information.

There must be restoration of her original vision and mission to be fulfilled by the removal of the bogus and illegal organizational structure established by individuals who are misleading the congregants by reinstating the founding family.

"...And if the blind lead the blind, both shall fall into the ditch. Matthew 15:14"

Steven and I, have been pursuing justice since our Mom passed. We have honored our commitment, responsibility and duty to carry the mantle office and the ministry forward with knowledge, respect and preservation.

The Legacy and vision of our founder is clear.

Allen and Via took over the (2) physical buildings owned by the church. The few parishioners that had not yet left; Via told them they had to change the locks on the front door. Via and Allen said to the few parishioners that they had to change the locks because Steven and me were coming back to burgurize the church.

Our God given mandate from God is to carry the vision and legacy forward. After being ignored by the defendants we file a civil suit in the Supreme Court of New York.

The courts advised and asked us to try and work out a settlement agreement to resolve our issues before litigation. The defendants best resolution to a settlement was: "Steven and I could attend church services as visitors...And maybe someday we might get voted into our church positions again. Mind you Steve is an ordained minister by the church, and Administrator. My title is Director of Church Corporate Affairs. In addition, I am a lifetime Trustee Board Member of the church.

After four years, the defendants continue to stonewall, and are still deficient with answering our interrogatories and remain non-compliant to the court proceedings. For example, they refuse to give access to church financial records, or other church records that Steven and I have standing to view all church records...the church is a 5013c non-profit corporation.

If you are so compelled please feel free to visit our Facebook Page for a complete and full accounting and comprehension of real-time events of our civil suit from start to finish.

At this time we extend our gratitude and appreciation for your prayers, well wishes, and unyielding support to our endeavor to follow through on What we are called to do.

I admonish and encourage church goers and non-church goers; return back to reading our Bibles.

In honor and love we celebrate the Legacy of (Apostle) Reverend Elizabeth Alston. We acknowledge her life of tireless service to God and humanity.

Apostle Alston's service spanned over five decades. We celebrate her life, her legacy, her vision. The life and memory of Reverend Elizabeth Alston, will live on being more than just a slogan of: "We will never forget you."

The legacy of Reverend Elizabeth Alston, the Founder and Pastor of St. John Deliverance Tabernacle Church; will remain unyielding to the fading away into obscurity. Our Mom's sacrifice, and our family's sacrifice has been enormous.

I sincerely thank you for reading, "Churches Incorporated."

No one holds the distinction to be perfect. Mistakes are not a life sentence. Mistakes allow us to be human through God's eyes.

Isiah 64

"All of us have become like one who is unclean, and all our righteous acts are like filthy rags; we all shrivel up like a leaf, and like the wind our sins sweep us away. No one calls on your name or strives to lay hold of you; for you have hidden your face from us and made us waste away because of our sins." Isaiah 64:6 (KJV)

"But we are all as an unclean thing, and all our righteousnesses are as filthy rags; and we all do fade as a leaf; and our iniquities, like the wind, have taken us away."

I prefer, rather than saying Reverend Alston has passed away. I say, thank God for Reverend Elizabeth Alston, passing our way...

At this time we extend our gratitude and appreciation for your prayers, well wishes, and unyielding support to our endeavor to follow through on what we are called to do.

I sincerely thank you for reading, "Churches Incorporated."

ABOUT THE AUTHOR

MR. ALSTON RESIDES IN STONY Point, New York. He is a three-time award-winning author for his book titled *No More Mr. Nice Guy*. Mr. Alston is a recipient of the humanitarian award and the author of *A Lost Art: Business Etiquette with Exceptional Service*. Shortly after college he started his career in executive management. James E. Alston was born in the rural setting of Franklin County, North Carolina, the oldest of three children. His family relocated to New York in 1957. Mr. Alston is the son of a pastor and has held various church board positions. Most recent was pastor of church administration and church corporate affairs.

9 781960 946027